The Ultimate Unauthorized
Eragon Guide

Also by Lois H. Gresh

Dragonball Z

The Truth Behind a Series of Unfortunate Events

The Science of Supervillains

The Science of Superheroes

The Termination Node

Chuck Farris and the Tower of Darkness

Chuck Farris and the Labyrinth of Doom

Chuck Farris and the Cosmic Storm

Technolife 2020

The Computers of Star Trek

The Science of Anime

The Science of James Bond

The Fan's Guide to the Spiderwick Chronicles*

Exploring Philip Pullman's His Dark Materials*

*Forthcoming

The Ultimate Unauthorized Eragon Guide

The Hidden Facts Behind the World of Alagaësia

Lois H. Gresh

ST. MARTIN'S GRIFFIN

NEW YORK

www.stmartins.com

Library of Congress Cataloging-in-Publication Data

Gresh, Lois H.
    The ultimate unauthorized Eragon guide : the hidden facts behind the world of Alagaësia /
Lois Gresh.—1st. ed.
        p. cm.
    Includes bibliographical references.
    ISBN-13: 978-0-312-35792-4
    ISBN-10: 0-312-35792-3
    1. Paolini, Christopher. Inheritance—Handbooks, manuals, etc.—Juvenile literature. 2.
Fantasy fiction, American—Handbooks, manuals, etc.—Juvenile literature. 3. Dragons in
literature—Handbooks, manuals, etc.—Juvenile literature. I. Title.

PS3616.A55I5434 2006
813'.6—dc22

                                                                          2006040045

10 9 8 7 6 5 4 3 2

Contents

The Ultimate Unauthorized Eragon Guide

· 1 ·
So What's It All About?

I'm a jaded old science fiction and fantasy writer, ancient enough to be Christopher Paolini's mother. Imagine my surprise to learn that at the age of twenty, Paolini had sold over one million copies of his first fantasy novel, *Eragon*. How did this happen, I wondered, and is the book any good?

I rushed out to my local bookstore and grabbed (well, bought) a copy of *Eragon*.[1] Weighing in at 503

---

1. Christopher Paolini, *Eragon* (New York: Alfred A. Knopf, 2003).

pages, the novel featured a dragon on the front cover and the prestigious announcement that *Eragon* was "The #1 *New York Times* Best-seller." Totally impressed (remember, I'm a jaded old writer with seventeen books to my name, and I've never sold one million copies of anything), I flipped to the acknowledgments in the back of the book. Here, I learned from Paolini's notes that he began writing *Eragon* when he was fifteen years old and that his parents' publishing company, Paolini International, LLC, first published *Eragon* in 2002. His mother arranged book signings throughout the United States, and at one of these events, Paolini met Michelle Frey, now his editor at Knopf Books. The rest is history: *USA Today* best-seller, *New York Times* best-seller, an upcoming movie called *Eragon* being released from Twentieth Century Fox in December of 2006, a second book called *Eldest* with a first print run of one million copies, and a young author with many millions of fans around the world.

Immediately, I returned to the front of the book and started reading.

Now I assume that you, the reader of *this* book, have

already read both *Eragon* and its sequel, *Eldest*.[2] If you haven't read these two books in Christopher Paolini's Inheritance trilogy, then I urge you to race to the bookstore and buy copies right away. Of course, if your school or local library has copies, then you can check out the books rather than buy them. The important thing is to read the books because they're a lot of fun. My guess is that schools are letting kids read the Inheritance books for English class, so you may actually get copies simply by going to school and attending class.

So what's it all about, this world of *Eragon* and *Eldest*? And why is it so popular?

Basically, the series concerns a teenager whose name happens to be Eragon. At the age of fifteen, Eragon is living with his uncle Garrow and working on the farm, wondering about the identities of his real parents. His mother, Selena, may still be alive. She left when Eragon was born. And his father is totally unknown to him.

Clearly, when a book opens the possibility that someone's mother may still be alive, she'll probably

---

2. Christopher Paolini, *Eldest* (New York: Alfred A. Knopf, 2005).

show up somewhere before the series ends. It's like the old smoking gun: if a novel, play, or movie has a smoking gun sitting on the mantel of a fireplace (or elsewhere) in the opening act, there'd better be a reason for the gun later on!

As for the "totally unknown" father, this is another smoking gun. We expect Eragon's father to show up at some point, to be someone powerful (think Darth Vader or a king, major magician, or major good guy), and to either create enormous obstacles for Eragon or to help him. At minimum, we expect to find out if he's dead or alive; same for Eragon's mother.

At any rate, Eragon likes to wander around a no-man's land, a dense mountain range called the Spine, and there he finds a blue stone that happens to be a dragon's egg. Out pops a baby dragon, later named Saphira, and she bonds with Eragon, making him the first Dragon Rider in a very long time.

It seems that thousands of years ago, elves and dragons fought, and Dragon Riders brought peace to the land. Eragon's world is still packed with elves, dragons, black spells, dwarves, and magic of all kinds. There are bad guys, such as the evil king Galbatorix and the Ra'zac, some deadly beetlelike guys. Thrown into the mix are Angela, the herbalist and fortune-teller, and her werecat, Solembum. Eragon and Saphira use mental telepathy to communicate, and the elf princess Arya also uses mental telepathy to "talk to" Eragon.

The notion of Dragon Riders has been in other fantasy novels. For example, a book by Cornelia Funke is actually called *Dragon Rider.* In ancient China in the Han dynasty, people believed that immortal humans rode dragons. They considered dragons to be closely associated with clouds and the seas, lakes, and rivers.[3] If somebody was riding a dragon, it meant that he was in perfect harmony with nature, and hence, would live forever, which is what the word "immortal" means. In the famous *Lord of the Rings* by J. R. R. Tolkien, Frodo encounters a wraith who is riding a dragon. The examples of Dragon Riders are endless.

---

3. http://www.east-asian-history.net/textbooks/PM-China/graphics/Ch7/03.htm.

Anne McCaffrey, possibly the queen of dragon fantasy novels, wrote the famous *Dragonriders of Pern* series and explains on her Web site how she came up with the idea of dragons who are good guys with mental telepathy and deep, symbiotic relationships with humans. She says, "Back in 1967 . . . I had to develop a planet which needed a renewable airforce against some unknown menace and came up with Pern, dragons, Thread and humans who Impressed a hatching in a lifelong symbiotic relationship. Rather wonderful to have an intelligent partner that loves you unconditionally. Who wouldn't like a forty-foot telepathic dragon as their best friend?"[4]

In the *Dragonriders of Pern* novels (fourteen books have been published to date), Dragonriders are chosen because they are able to communicate telepathically with giant sentient dragons. The lifetime friendship and close bond between Dragonriders and dragons begins when the dragon hatches. Sound familiar to you? It's what happens in *Eragon* when Saphira hatches and bonds with the hero.

---

4. http://www.annemccaffrey.net/faq/index.html.

Even the folk song, "Puff the Magic Dragon,"[5] refers to a boy who is riding a dragon. In the song (I don't know about you, but my teachers made us sing "Puff the Magic Dragon" from kindergarten through sixth grade), "Jackie kept a lookout perched on Puff's gigantic tail."

The first book in Christopher Paolini's trilogy, *Eragon,* is filled with chases, kidnappings, adventures, sword fights, fistfights, dwarf kings, weird bald magicians, death, friendship, and love. It is a complete book, round and full of plots and subplots, dozens of characters, and dozens of places. It is what is commonly called an epic tale, one of vast proportions and sweeping storylines.

For me, one of the most fun aspects of *Eragon* is learning about Saphira, the dragon. Sure, dragons have been done before in fantasy books, over and over again. But when an author's really good, his presentation of dragons is unique. In *Eragon,* Saphira is lovable from the beginning, and readers can't help but enjoy watching her grow up alongside her human friend. At first, she cannot breathe fire or fly well. But she grows very

---

5. Written by Peter Yarrow and Leonard Lipton, 1963.

quickly, and soon, rather than standing as tall as Eragon's knees, she is an enormous beast the size of a plane. He makes a harness for her that will grow as she grows, and the description of the harness and how it is created is fascinating. Also of interest is how much Saphira eats. She could probably devour an entire herd of cattle as a midnight snack. And, finally, I really like the way Saphira devotes herself to Eragon. They are true friends. She genuinely cares about him—as much as a mother, close sister, or twin brother would care about him. In return, he is devoted to his dragon and hides her from anyone who could cause her harm. Together, they learn to fly and do good deeds, and this aspect of *Eragon*—the beautiful and intricate relationship between Eragon and Saphira—is my favorite part of the series.

As soon as *Eldest* was released on August 31, 2005, I raced out and bought a copy. I was anxious to find out more about Eragon and Saphira and their world. Would Eragon fall for the elf princess Arya? Would the Urgals kill more villagers? Would Galbatorix beat Eragon and maintain his evil control of all life in Eragon's world? And what about Saphira: would she stay safe, gain new powers, and remain with Eragon?

The second book, *Eldest,* is 681 pages long. I read the entire book during one weekend. I couldn't put it down.

Eldest begins with a lengthy summary of what happened in *Eragon,* so in case you've forgotten some details, you can quickly catch up and read the next part of the adventure.

In the second novel, Eragon becomes far more elflike and this is useful, given that he's falling in love with elf princess Arya. The Urgals have killed nearly all of the trolls, and Eragon must save everyone, including the elves and dwarves. He studies at length with the dwarves and learns more magic and battle techniques. We encounter a sorceress, Trianna, meet up with Angela the herbalist again, and learn a lot about dwarves. Much of this dwarf information is from common folklore, just as many of the dragon details are commonly known and used by many other novelists. For example, the dwarves are miners who live primarily in caves and underground tunnels. In *Eldest,* we also learn that the land was once populated by giants and that the world was formed during an elaborate creation sequence, which we'll talk about later in this book.

There are dragon beasts, a white Poelike raven (don't worry, I'll tell you more about all of these subjects later), and even another dragon named Glaedr to befriend Saphira. We encounter a Menoa tree in the elf woods, and the tree is actually intelligent and alive in the manner that creatures are intelligent and alive. A baby blessed by Eragon has magical abilities and the mark of the dragon on her forehead. Possibly another Dragon Rider is growing up.

Basically, in *Eldest,* the story evolves through more adventures in which Eragon becomes more elflike and stronger in magic and his ability to bond with nature. Far more characters are introduced, including dwarves, dragons, dragon beasts, elves, and fairies. Issues about souls and flesh and wraiths and sorcerers are discussed, as well as even deeper matters, such as how the world itself was created. And in the end, we learn that Eragon is the son of Morzan. As a reminder, Morzan fought with the evil Galbatorix against the Dragon Riders. Murtagh was also one of Morzan's sons, but Murtagh denounced his father and fled from Galbatorix's evil ways.

Of course, there's a lot more to the story than the brief tidbits I am supplying here. Again, I'm assuming that you've already read both *Eragon* and *Eldest,* and now, you want to delve further into all the magic and fantasy.

This particular book—the one in your hands now—explores the magic, fantasy, and creatures behind *Eragon* and *Eldest.* We'll take a fun look at elves, dwarves, giants, and dragons, and we'll try to figure out what magic is and whether it really exists. We'll also explore dragon riders in the past, in folktales or stories by other famous writers. Have there been elves and dwarves that are similar to the ones in *Eragon* and *Eldest*? Is mental telepathy possible? Fortune-telling? Are plants sentient, meaning "do they think?" Is it possible to instantly transport fom one place to another, a process commonly known as teleportation? And can you cure illnesses and injuries using Angela's methods of herbalism?

These are only a few of the things we'll talk about in this book. And, all the while, we'll keep in mind what's happening to Eragon, the main character, and his companion, the fire-breathing dragon Saphira. By the way, have you noticed that the word "Eragon" is the same as the word "Dragon" except for the use of an initial *E* rather than a *D*? And have you also noticed that Saphira's name includes the word "fire" (phira)?

Here's something new that I learned while writing this book: did you know that many scientists believe that there were once feathered dinosaurs on Earth, and that the ancient people thought these gigantic feathered dinosaurs were dragons? Until I started thinking about *Eragon* and *Eldest,* I wasn't aware that dinosaurs somehow evolved in conjunction with birds—don't worry, I tell you all about this stuff in chapter 3, "*FIRE!* Saphira and the Dragons"—nor did I know much about how folklore beliefs about dragons started long ago.

Hopefully, you'll learn lots of new, interesting things in this book, which you can think of as an exploration of all things *Eragon* and *Eldest.* And hopefully, you'll have a great time learning all about famous folktales, dwarves, elves, and magical methods and will enjoy future books in the series and the movie that much more.

· 2 ·
What's the Point (of Those Ears)?
Eragon and the Elves

Pointy ears. Elves have 'em. Eragon has 'em. Does this mean that Eragon *is* an elf?

Maybe. Maybe not. Only Christopher Paolini knows for sure. But by the end of *Eldest,* we're pretty sure that Eragon has turned into an elf. He thinks he's an elf. He's in love with an elf. So he probably is an elf.

So, just what *is* an elf?

An elf is usually classified as a type of fairy, and these fantasy creatures are found in everything from fairy tales—gee, there's a surprise!—to the *Lord of the*

Rings to J. K. Rowling's books and even to the old English theatrical works of William Shakespeare, a very famous playwright that you will study in high school.

In *Eragon,* we're told that a young elf killed a dragon causing a war between elves and dragons. The war raged for many years, and then finally another elf, this one named Eragon but not *our* Eragon, discovered the egg of a dragon. He let it hatch and befriended the baby dragon, raising the beast and teaching the world to live in harmony. Dragons, man, and elves all lived in peace for a very long time, and to make sure the peace held, Dragon Riders roamed the land.[1]

In J. R. R. Tolkien's the *Lord of the Rings* trilogy, a human named Aragorn (kind of close to Eragon, don't you think?) forges an alliance between elves and mankind, and together they defeat evil. Like Paolini's Eragon, Tolkien's Aragorn has amazing magical skills and is able to summon and unite bonds ranging back to the dawn of time. Aragorn's father died when he was a baby, and his mentor over the years is an elf-lord

---

1. Paolini, *Eragon,* p. 50.

named Elrond. It's interesting to note that Eragon's father is unknown to him from infancy and that Eragon learns his skills from an elf master as well.

In the Tolkien tales, Aragorn's true identity, that he is a direct descendant of Elendil, who founded kingdoms, as well as Elros Tar-Minyatur, first king of Numenor, is kept secret for a very long time. In fact, his true identity is kept so secret that he doesn't learn about his ancestry until he grows up. Eragon's true identity is also kept secret for many years, so secret that he does not know his ancestry until he is a young man.

As a young man, Tolkien's Aragorn falls in love with Arwen, half-elf queen of the Reunited Kingdom of Arnor and Gondor. Arwen is as beautiful as her ancestor Luthien Tinuviel, the most beautiful of all elves. To parallel, Paolini's Eragon falls in love with the beautiful elf princess, Arya. Aragorn and Arwen, Eragon and Arya: the names and the general relationships are very similar.

According to the Tolkien tales, elves are the first inhabitants of a place called Middle Earth and are the most beautiful, fair, and wise creatures of the land. They love songs, dancing, and art, and their senses

Santa Claus and His Elves

Of all the elves in all the fairy tales around the world, which elves might be the most famous to readers of this book? I thought about this little puzzle for a long time. Then I remembered that Santa Claus uses elves at Christmastime.

According to the story, Santa and Mrs. Claus live at the North Pole. With them are many elves, who create all sorts of toys and goodies for kids to get on Christmas morning.

Santa is also known as Saint Nick, Kris Kringle, and Father Christmas. He actually comes from an ancient European folk story that was based on a real person named St. Nicholas of Myra, a fourth-century bishop from Byzantine Anatolia, or present-day Turkey. St. Nicholas gave gifts to impoverished people, which is how the giving of gifts to children on

Christmas Day was started. The name Santa Claus comes from the Dutch word *Sinterklaas,* which crosses the two notions of St. Nicholas the bishop and Father Christmas, who first emerged as a character in the 1600s in Britain. In the old days, Father Christmas didn't wear red robes. Rather, he wore green robes lined in fur.

As the tale grew, people began to think that Santa created all the toys himself up there at the North Pole. That's a lot of work for one guy to do! So, people figured poor Santa had to have some help. Rather than give Santa factories, people preferred to think of elves making all those toys—but still by hand, crafting each toy with great care and devotion.

exceed those of humans. They are skilled at what humans think of as magic.

In actuality, elves are derived from folklore around the world, most commonly from mythical creatures of northern Europe. They are basically a type of fairy, possessing great beauty, magic skill, heightened senses, and wisdom. There are deviations, of course, in various folktales and modern fantasies, but this description of elves is probably the most standard one.

If elves are a type of fairy, which they are, I wonder where all the other kinds of fairies are living in Eragon's world. Where are the brownies, pixies, gnomes, and goblins?

I happen to believe in fairies. I also believe in angels and the possibility that there's an opening to another universe in my closet. Now don't laugh! I can't prove that fairies, angels, and openings to other universes don't exist. Nobody can prove that these things don't exist, anymore than we can prove that there's no such thing as ghosts, witches, and demons. So, who's to say that they *don't* exist? Because there's no proof in either direction—either that they exist, or that they don't exist—I figure there's a strong possibility that fairies, angels, ghosts, and other traditionally supernatural beings are out there, floating around, flying, flitting, dancing, singing, and living in worlds that we don't even know about. Consider that there was a time when we didn't know about quantum particles, which are the tiny (invisible) parts of everything around us. Consider that there was a time when we didn't know about cells, much less the human brain, the heart, and most anything about our own bodies. It wasn't that long ago, perhaps one hundred to one hundred fifty years. In another one hundred to one hundred fifty years, we may know a lot more about the world around us than we know now. We may discover that there are indeed fairies and angels, and maybe even ghosts and ghouls, where we can't see them yet.

There's a woman named Gossamer Penwyche (which you must admit is one of the most beautiful names you've ever heard), and in her book, *The World of Fairies,* she writes, "I believe in fairies. My belief is based on a simple, childlike faith that I have never lost and a childhood experience I have never forgotten." When Penwyche was a little girl playing in a stream near her house, she saw fairies for the first time. While she was daydreaming with her legs floating in the water, the wind picked up and blew around her like a mini tornado, birds started chirping, a hawk screamed then grew quiet. Gossamer Penwyche heard children's laughter and singing, but when she looked around, nobody was there. The hawk dove at her face, and she fell into the water, only to hear the children laughing more loudly, presumably at her. She eventually realized that hours had passed rather than minutes and that she'd just experienced a spell of intense magic. She was certain she'd heard the laughter and songs of fairies.[2]

But that's just one person. Have other people encountered fairies, perhaps even met them?

Famous fairy artist Sulamith Wulfing writes, "My ideas come to me from many sources, and in such harmony with my personal experiences that I can turn them into these fairy compositions."[3]

---

2. Gossamer Penwyche, *The World of Fairies* (New York: Sterling Publishing Company, 2001), pp. 6–7.

3. David Larkin, *The Fantastic Art of Sulamith Wulfing* (New York: Peacock/Bantam, 1978), quoted at http://www.bpib.com/wulfing.htm.

Fairies are usually shown in books and paintings as tiny winged people with the ability to do magical things. They're kind and playful. We all know about the tooth fairy, for example, who flutters like a tiny winged angel into our bedrooms at night and gives us coins (or other small gifts) for teeth placed under our pillows. The fairy godmother, on the other hand, is often depicted as a human-sized winged elderly woman of great kindness.

Belief in fairies is as old as mankind. Some people believe that fairies are former gods and goddesses whose power diminished over time. This is why fairies are so tiny, these people claim. Other people say that fairies are the spirits of the dead. They point to the fact that the word "sprite," which is a name often given to fairies, is very similar to the word "spirit."

Around the world, various religions point to fairies as angels who were rejected from heaven but weren't evil enough for hell. In addition to the Old and New Testaments, commonly known as the Bible, angels are found in the Book of Mormon, the Koran, and the Dead Sea Scrolls.

According to many religions, Satan refused to give into God's power and authority. Instead, he grabbed a third of God's angels, throwing them into a war with all the angels of God's light, including the most powerful good-guy angel, the one known as the archangel Michael. This is a well-known story and has even been made into movies such as Christopher Walken's Prophecy trilogy. Supposedly, the angels who sided with Satan were thrown out of heaven to live on Earth. As the story goes, these angels weren't really evil. They were just misguided and misunderstood. So they weren't killed; rather, they were cast from heaven down to Earth to live among mortals. Some of the lesser angels, poor misguided souls, got caught up in the battle, and being of such minute power (compared to archangels and Satan, et cetera), they went along with the crowd, their crowd being the angels who sided with Satan. These lesser angels became the fairy tribes.

Falling down to Earth, they discovered beautiful things such as trees, grass, flowers, and butterflies, and everything about nature fascinated them. The lesser angels, or fairies, liked humans, and saw people as part of nature itself. Everyone would work together, humans and fairies, to make a nice world. Of course, some fairies were bitter and hid in caves and dark tunnels beneath the ground, blaming the humans for their fall from grace. While these darker fairies didn't actively try to destroy mankind, they really didn't care about people, either. They figured that among his many (trillions of) sins, Satan refused to bow before humanity. Perhaps this was a reason for the war between the angels, and perhaps this was a reason why the fairies were cast out of heaven. So, these darker fairies grumbled, griped, and snarled a lot.

In areas of the world where people roamed, people believed that fairies might have been pygmy natives. This is how the Celtic people came to think that fairies lived in the hills called fairy mounds. The pygmies didn't quite trust the large-sized humans and tended to run and hide from them. Hence, the notion arose that they were burrowing into the ground through hidden entrances. The large-sized humans fascinated the fairies, so they began to mimic many of the activities that they saw humans doing. For example, this is why fairies began to dance, sing, and throw parties . . . or so the legend goes.

Don't worry, I'm building back up to Eragon and his elves. If you know something about fairies and elves, which are a type of fairy, then you'll start to see where a lot of *Eragon*'s folklore comes from.

For the most part, people have believed that fairies are simple spirits of nature, not fallen angels. These spirits are manifestations of animal and human souls and thoughts. This means that the fairies are created from some essence of our spirits that is everywhere at all times.

In the 1400s, a man named Paracelsus classified fairies into four groups, which became known as elementals. The fairies who live in the air are called *sylphs*. Those who live on earth are *gnomes*. The underwater fairies are called *undines,* and finally, the fairies who deal with fire are the *salamanders*. In addition to the four elementals, there are also many other nature spirits, such as the ice spirit known as Jack Frost.

How to See Elves: A Recipe

Along with all the stories *about* elves, there are stories about how to attract them. Say you really want to see what Fairy Land is like, or you want to find someone like Eragon or Arya to pal around with. How might you go about doing this?

First, you have to be able to see elves if you want to hang out with them. But they're not exactly visible to us, are they? Luckily, recipes exist for making elves visible.

Before using the recipes, go into the forest, somewhere quiet, where you might find elves. Make sure there are plenty of mushrooms around where the elves might sit and dream in the sun. If you can find a quiet forest spot with tall cool trees and plenty of flowers and mushrooms, you're halfway to Fairy Land. If you happen to show up at the crack of dawn or the stroke of midnight, your chances are even higher for seeing elves. Now, don't do any of this without dragging your parents with you. It's not a good idea to go into the deep forest all alone at midnight or the crack of dawn. If your father is living at home with you and he happens to be six foot six and looks like one of those World Wrestling Federation muscle men, then maybe you can trek into the midnight forest clinging to the back of his shirt, holding on for dear life, and letting him lead the way.

Well, all that aside, I'm just telling you the most ideal conditions possible for seeing elves. You'll have to modify these conditions to suit reality.

Okay, so you're in the middle of the forest as the sun rises, sitting in a pile of mushrooms and flowers. You're not carrying any iron, of course, because fairies can't *stand* iron. So, make sure to leave all your rusty necklaces and heavy chains at home. Look for a stone with a big hole in the middle of it. The stone should look like a doughnut. If you find one, plop down on the mushrooms next to it.

Continuing this make-believe scenario, you take a vial of special fairy ointment out of your pocket. You should prepare this ointment in advance and carry it with you at all times. If a teacher finds the vial on you, tell the truth, as in "No, Captain Major Smithies (I'm assuming your teacher doubles as an army captain), these aren't drugs in the vial. This is my fairy ointment, and I smear it on my eyelids so I can see fairies." Got it? This is good advice (but remember, this is just make-believe). It's better if Captain Major Smithies think you're nuts than if he thinks you're committing major crimes.

I suppose you want that fairy ointment recipe now, don't you? Gather the buds of thyme, marigold, hazel flowers (very important ingredient), and hollyhocks, and crush them with four-leaf clovers. Add vegetable oil to the mixture. Finally add the secret ingredients. When all the buds and clovers are in a thick paste, you have fairy ointment and you can cram the slimy mixture into a vial. I should add that, if you pick the flower buds when the moon is full, they'll be better at revealing fairies. Also note that the longer you let the ointment sit in a dark room, the more powerful it becomes. So if you were really doing this (which, of course, you're not), put the ointment in your basement or in a damp locker room that happens to be three stories under the school gym—the damper the better—and *then* trek out to the forest, smear the ointment on your eyelids, and see what happens.

You'll probably see something. If it's a fairy, don't blink or it will disappear. If it's not a fairy, then you're probably going blind from smearing musty, fungus-dripping, moldy, rotting clover bud paste on your eyelids.

Personally, I'd rather *not* see fairies if I have to use this ointment. I'm also not a fan of adventures in the woods at dawn or midnight. But if you really want to do this stuff, like I said, get your father, Paul Bunyan, and maybe a bunch of burly woodsmen uncles to go with you.

Because elves are a type of gnome, we'll talk about them last. First, we'll delve briefly into the other three elementals.

The air elementals, or sylphs, rule the skies and cause the winds to blow. They make the clouds and the snow, and they tend to be tempestuous, just like the weather. The sylphs are musical beings, because after all, they hear everything that floats through the breezes. They represent our minds to some extent because they breathe inspiration into our souls from the greater universe they inhabit. Hence, it is often thought by those who believe in fairies that the sylphs, and the air itself, represent the mind. As such, they can cause dreams, and within humans and animals, they work within the realms of the nervous system, where the brain is located.

The fire elementals, or salamanders, are directly responsible for fire: without the elementals, fire cannot be created. These creatures embody all of the fiery aspects of our personalities. They are fearless and their will is strong. They are the essence of raw spirit. Within humans and animals, they work within the realms of the bloodstream and the liver, and they affect human emotions. Salamanders either look like lizards or tiny balls of light in the middle of a flame. You probably don't want to play around with them.

Let's suppose you see a red and orange lizard zipping around your backyard. The lizard scoots up a tree, then falls and hops onto your big toe. It plays dead. (Lizards do this, I know, because I used to live in California, and there were lizards all over our backyard, playing dead for our cat.) So, here's this lizard, presumably dead, and it's on your big toe. Like a total bozo, you don't flick the lizard off your foot. Instead, you take a nap. Along comes your friend, Justin, and he's in a really bad mood. Justin has just broken up with his girl-friend, Brittany—or wait a minute, maybe that was a different Justin—and he's yelling about the whole thing. Naturally, you wake up. You blink. Justin is two yards away from you, throwing fruit from your lemon tree at the fence across the yard. Now, he switches to peaches. He's making a huge mess. You have the lizard . . . or rather, the salamander elemental . . . on your big toe. You get up angrily, shake your foot, hop-ing to knock off the lizard. You say, "Stop throwing my mother's peaches against the fence! She's gonna kill me!" The lizard flips into the air then opens its mouth really wide and half swallows your big toe, hanging on to your foot for dear life. "Ouch! Get outta here!" Now, you're yelling at Justin *and* the lizard. Justin thinks you're yelling at him to leave. He starts calling you stupid names. In the meantime, you're getting increasingly angry, too, and the lizard is just having a good ol' time, because he's inflamed two friends against each other. If he's a really powerful lizard, maybe Justin will even go up in flames.

Moral of the story: be careful with salamanders.

The water elementals are made up of the undines, water sprites, mermaids, sea nymphs, and such strange-sounding creatures as limoniades, nereides, potamides, oreades, and naiads. They live in all the oceans, seas, rivers, lakes, creeks, and other watery places. Because water has such a calming and connecting power over people, the undines possess those qualities as well. They calm people and they are highly empathetic, meaning they understand how we feel, connect us to one another, and soothe our complex relationships and difficulties.

People believe that a water elemental guards each fountain, each creek, each spurt of water. They're physically beautiful beings, usually considered female, and they often take on human form to communicate and interact with people.

But let's get to those elves, shall we? They are part of the fourth and final group of fairy elementals known as the gnomes.

The gnomes represent the earth elemental and are fascinated by the processes through which matter transforms. The gnomes may be driads, hamadriads (or tree spirits), brownies, elves, satyrs, pans, or goblins. They're concerned mainly with rocks, stones, plants, minerals, and gems. Magicians tend to work closely with gnomes so they can learn more about how to transform one metal to another, manipulate an object so it moves elsewhere, and so forth.

As nature spirits, elves are part of the earth elemental force. In *Eragon,* the elves give new Dragon Riders special swords. The method of forging the special swords is a big secret. This makes sense when we consider that elves, who are commonly considered to be gnomes, are greatly concerned with the transformation of natural materials. Forging requires transformation of the material used to create the special swords. In fact, Eragon's sword, known as Zar'roc, is iridescent and ripples like water when Saphira touches it. Clearly, Zar'roc possesses magical ability of some kind and is made from a magical form of metal.

Elves are guardians of natural places like the deep forest. They protect nature and all the creatures of the wilderness. The elves are truly the Fair Folk and are finer in character, substance, and ability than people. Their eyes slant softly, they have pointed ears, they are extremely intelligent. Because they are highly skilled in all things related to nature and magic, they can see spiritual things all around them as if the spirits are vibrating in the air. They are smaller than humans and more delicate in form. In addition, they live in societies in which a king and queen preside, and their communities hold parties to mark the various seasons and the forces of nature.

How close is this folktale description to the elves in *Eragon*? Keep in mind that this is the standard way of

How to Attract Elves: A Recipe

If you made it past the recipe for seeing elves, then you're a bonafide, hardcore elf hound, and you're ready to smear on the ointments that actually attract elves *to* you.

A word of warning here: you will look ridiculous and you will smell funny. Be advised that your friends will laugh at you, if indeed you still have any friends after smearing these ointments on yourself, and you may get thrown out of school. So, check with religious leaders, your school principal, at least three dozen burly uncles who happen to be woodsmen, and at least one grandmother and your mother before proceeding. And then still don't do it.

Step 1. Smear amber tree resin on your wrists. Exercise caution, as amber may attract dwarves as well as elves. You could have a pack of cantankerous little men following you to math class tomorrow.

Step 2. Smear honeysuckle sap all over your cheeks. Woodland fairies will flock to you. On the other hand, bees may flock to you, as well, so be careful.

Step 3. Drench your hair in lemon juice. Ignore your friends as they start to call you Fruit Loops, while pointing at you and laughing. What do they know? If they bothered to smear themselves in amber and honeysuckle and pour buckets of lemon juice on their heads, well then, they might get to see elves, too!

Step 4. Rub a paste of sandalwood, patchouli, roses, and pine essence all over your arms and feet. The sandalwood will tell elves that you believe in shape shifting and magic healing. The patchouli tells them that you're full of belief and compassion for the elf ways. The rose is an elf favorite, and few elves can ignore the aroma of strong roses. And finally, the pine essence will draw the elves near because they are always drawn to anything that reminds them of the deep forest.

Now, I'm always cautioning you (I'm *sure* you've noticed), saying things like "ask your preachers, teachers, parents, and principals first" and "bring fourteen burly firemen with you." Why do I give you all these warnings? Let's just put it this way: if you want to smear all kinds of smelly pastes on your body and dump lemon juice over your head, don't call me if something goes wrong. Just make sure to ask everyone who matters before you try to attract elves. Ask the head of the international medical doctors' society.[4] Ask the president of the United States. Ask Tony Blair, Prime Minister of England. Ask every king, queen, president, and prime minister in the world. And get the personal okay of Christopher Paolini. Then you might be safe to proceed.

---

4. There is no such society. I made it up.

describing elves in fairy folklore books and spoken tales around the world.

It's very close, isn't it?

In *Eragon,* Arya is the princess of all elves and her mother is Queen Islanzadi. Eragon is in love with her and basically transforms into an elf over the course of the first two books, *Eragon* and *Eldest.* Both Arya and Eragon have pointed ears, softly slanted eyes, and great intelligence. In fact, Eragon shrinks physically to appear more elflike as his transformation from human to elf takes place. By the end of *Eldest,* Eragon is seeing spirits and vibrations in the air all around him.

In fact, in *Eldest,* Eragon literally steps into Fairy Land, which I'll describe more in a minute. Saphira tells Eragon that the forest is alive and that the elves have more magic than humans, dwarves, or anyone else. Eragon finds that the elves are more beautiful than humans, and indeed, his own hair takes on an elf luster, shimmering "like the finest wire in the sun."[5] He goes so far as to tell himself that he looks like a

---

5. Paolini, *Eldest,* pp. 168–214.

princeling, and we're told that even his skin emits "a faint glow, as if with the sheen of magic."[6]

Just as in our real world, where folklore scholars call elves the Fair Folk, the elves are known as Fair Folk in the world of Eragon. In *Eldest*, Oromis tells Eragon that elves are called Fair Folk because they love beauty so much. They strive to look exactly perfect: each elf, perfect for him or herself, that is. Their magic enables them to modify even living things—not only the matter of the forest, the rocks, the minerals.[7]

And here's another parallel between the elves in Eragon's world and our real world: only the elves in Eragon's world know their own names.

The actual word "fairy" or "faerie" or "fayerie" comes from the ancient French word *faes*, which in turn, is derived from the Latin word *fata*. A long time ago, way back in the thirteenth century or so, people used the word "fairy" to describe all of the spiritual entities that had been in the folktales of the world for as

6. Paolini, *Eldest*, p. 471.
7. Paolini, *Eldest*, p. 391.

long as anyone could remember. The word, be it "fairy" or "faerie" or "fayerie," indicates that the spiritual entity was in a constant state of enchantment, that the entity could bring blessings to people, or possibly bring curses upon them. Because the people of long ago were afraid to anger the fairies who might cast the curses, they never uttered the names of any of the fairies. They simply called all of them fairies. Or collectively, they called them all the Fair Folk, the Good People, and other very similar things. Only the elves knew their own names.

In the 1800s in our real world, people called Spiritualists divided the fairies into two types. The first type consisted of nature spirits, who were tied to trees, rivers, forests, lakes, and other forms of nature. The second type consisted of angel-like fairies, who dwelled somewhere between thought and matter.

In the early 1900s, Charles W. Leadbeater took Charles Darwin's theory of evolution and used it to classify the fairies the same way that scientists classify animals and plants. He wrote that Fairy Land consists of seven distinct areas and that fairies occupied England before humans lived there. According to Leadbeater, humans took over England and drove out the fairies, who evolved in order to cope. In fact, they evolved from water up through fungi and bacteria and further through reptiles, birds, and eventually, to the spiritual plane. At this spiritual level, as full mature fairies, they were linked to the air, earth, water, and fire. Even as full mature fairies, they continued to evolve until they were indeed like angels and existed as solar spirits.

Other ideas about fairies lived alongside the ideas that the creatures were angels, spirits, and similar to humans. For example, some people believed that fairies were like butterflies and made from something that's even lighter than air. This is why fairies are invisible except as the mere twinkling of light. These people thought that fairies linked plants and sunlight. If not for fairies, plants couldn't grow.

Even medical doctors had their notions about fairies. Franz Hartmann, for example, believed that fairies lived inside people as well as throughout nature. Fairies helped our bodies function correctly.

Long ago, the Welsh people thought that Fairy Land was north of them in the mountains. Later, they thought that Fairy Land was on a rocky peninsula, and still later, they believed that the fairies were on an island. Sailors would see the island and then at later times claim that the island had disappeared. British people called this place the Isle of Man. The Irish called it Hy Breasail.

Of all the fairy islands, Avalon is the best known for it was to Avalon that King Arthur was taken when he was mortally wounded. The story of King Arthur and the knights of his round table is very well known.

When Eragon steps into Fairy Land, he enters a place and time quite different from our own, yet existing alongside our world. His senses are heightened in Fairy Land, just as folklore scholars believe that people's senses are heightened in the real world if they find and enter Fairy Land.

People have theorized that Fairy Land is behind a natural doorway somewhere—maybe in my closet? Maybe in yours? In fact, in the famous Chronicles of Narnia fantasy stories by C. S. Lewis, it's suggested that there are doorways between the dimensions, possibly through a wardrobe. In the seven Narnia books, a huge struggle takes place in a magical world of humans, dwarves, witches, and other creatures. The Narnia books caused a lot of people to start wondering whether our world does indeed contain doors to other worlds. Could it be that entrances to Fairy Land are bored into mounds of earth or hollow hillsides?

Where earth energies are strong, people theorize that we might find the entrances into Fairy Land, which actually is another dimension of our own universe. Built in approximately 3500 B.C. at Carnac in Brittany, there are thousands of huge prehistoric stones in a precise configuration with dolmens at the ends of every row of stones. Dolmens are huge stone tables, or boulders, often associated with and piled up to form tombs. They are considered to be passage graves, or ways into the world of the dead. These passage graves, or portal dolmens, are gigantic and form actual doorways. It is commonly thought that these portals lead to Fairy Land.

As for Avalon, mentioned earlier, this island is part of a fairly complex folktale having to do with King Arthur. In short, there was an entrance to Fairy Land on Glastonbury Tor in Somerset, and a fairy king and lord of the Otherworld who went by the name Gwynn ap Nudd guarded this entrance. Gwynn ap Nudd lived in a palace inside the Tor with beautiful fairies surrounding his golden throne. This Nudd character was associated with King Arthur.

However, as time went on, the tale became increasingly complicated. Theories arose that the actual entrance to Fairy Land was somewhere across the sea. Hence, an island might be the way to Fairy Land. In particular, an island with ancient sites seemed like a good choice. Mont St. Michel was once considered the portal to Fairy Land, as was the Isle of Arran between Ireland and Scotland. In fact, the Isle of Arran was home to something called the Cauldron of Plenty, often considered by scholars to be the original Holy Grail.

Without getting into an elaborate discussion about this Holy Grail and what it was and what it had to do with Fairy Land, let's just say that all of this stuff was described in great detail in ancient poems. In these ancient poems were lavish descriptions of places that were just like Fairy Land. Of these places, one was called Avalon, or the sacred Isle of King Arthur.

Avalon was at Glastonbury. Today, Glastonbury Tor

is no longer an island. It is locked by the land, but still, it is surrounded in the distance by water.

Some fairy enthusiasts point out that the term *Elfame* (or *Elfhame,* meaning "Elf Home") was used rather than Fairy Land as long ago as the earliest Scottish folklore. The ways into Fairy Land are carefully guarded and based on laws devised by the fairies' Council of Elders and the Seelie Court.

According to legend, fairies live in two types of communities based on what they like to do and how they interact with humans. Peaceful fairies who mind their own business and don't cause much trouble for people reside in something known as the Seelie Court. They emerge in forests and fields to dance amongst the flowers and ferns, to feast, and to sing. Fairies who are dangerous to people and want to cause lots of trouble reside in the Unseelie Court ruled by the dark queen Nicnivin. These types of fairies live in the true wilderness and should be avoided at all cost.

As for elves, Scandinavian legends tell of Light Elves, the Liosalfar, who live high in the sky and are compassionate and kind. The Dark Elves, on the other hand, or Dockalfar, live beneath the ground and are nasty creatures. According to standard fairy lore, elves are pretty tall compared to most fairies, who are so small we can barely see them. Elves stand from four foot ten to five foot eight or more. They're slim and delicate with huge eyes of beautiful colors.

According to further folklore, Light Elves are seen only in special places where nature is undisturbed. They play music and they love art. Older elves are wiser and even more delicate and beautiful than younger elves. The elves are calm and patient, and they live for a very long time. All of these descriptions of Light Elves in "real life" could just as easily be descriptions of elves in *Eragon*.

The fact that elves in *Eragon* and *Eldest* follow our ancient folklore doesn't diminish our enjoyment of the novels. If anything, it deepens some readers' interest in Christopher Paolini's books. People find it interesting to see what new stories bring to the ancient folklore, and it's also fun to read great adventures featuring strong main characters such as Eragon.

· 3 ·
FIRE!
Saphira and the Dragons

Who's big, scaly, ferocious, and cuddly, all at the same time? And did I mention that she breathes fire and can probably eat a herd of antelopes for a mid-morning snack?

Obviously, I'm talking about Saphira, my favorite character in *Eragon* and *Eldest*. She's sweet, loyal, brilliant, and funny. She's like your dog, only better. She can talk to you through mental telepathy. Saphira is the ultimate pet/companion.

Very early in *Eragon*, our hero (whose name is also

Eragon) likes to hear troubadors telling stories about magic and the Dragon Riders.[1] He settles back and enjoys the troubadors' songs about dragons who guarded humans for thousands of years, and about our allies, the elves and dwarves. Then the Dragon Riders, great noble men, fell prey to King Galbatorix, who learned dark magic from a weird guy called the Shade. Galbatorix stole a black dragon hatchling, and then he and the Dragon Rider Morzan gathered a group of Dragon Riders and blazed off to kill all other Dragon Riders and elves. There was a huge war, the dragons were killed, and with them, the Dragon Riders.

This is the story that Eragon enjoys hearing. It's not a pretty story. It's gruesome and depressing, actually. But it also tells of adventures and bold, honorable men called Dragon Riders. It tells of the beloved, loyal dragons who lived for centuries. So, it makes sense that Eragon enjoys the story because it gives him a feeling of adventure and great longing.

---

1. In fact, Eragon is looking forward to hearing Dragon Rider stories as early as page 27 of *Eragon*.

Along comes Saphira. Eragon finds her shell and she hatches and then blows on him, filling him with dragon kinship and fire. There's a white oval on his palm, and he can feel the touch of her mind in his. It happens that quickly. Later, she touches the sword that will be called Ra'zac, and her touch sends the metal shimmering with iridescent colors. Basically, she gives magical abilities to the sword.

The dragon purrs, she snuggles against Eragon, and puffs of smoke rise from her nostrils as she sleeps. It's a lovely image, like that of a boy and his cat. Immediately, we like Saphira as if she's the perfect pet, companion, and friend.

Let's take a look at dragons, in general: just what are they and where do they come from? Are they real?

The dragon of *fantasy* is just that: it *is* a *fantasy*. However, it's not as if a knight was weak from starvation and dizzy from twenty-five days in 105-degree heat, and he saw visions and thought his horse was a winged, fire-breathing monster. It's not as if a caveman conked himself on the head with a stone mallet, and as he passed out, thought he saw a scaled monster with a pointed tail.

The Earliest Humans

Remember, the flying dinosaurs lived between 65 and 135 million years ago. The first humans (as far as we know) existed approximately 3.5 million years ago.

Anthropologists have found the oldest human skeletons in Hadar, Olduvai, Leatoli, and other locations in East Africa. A famous skeleton is called Lucy, and scientists have been able to piece about 40 percent of her back together from her fossils. She was an Australopithecus, an earlier version of human who lived before *Homo habilis, Homo erectus,* and then *Homo sapiens.*

Fantastic as they are, dragons do have a basis in long-ago reality. For example, around 65 million years ago (I did say *long-ago* reality), a giant pterosaur (which means "winged reptile" in Greek) called the Quetzalcoatlus soared through the air like a giant dragon. This pterosaur had a really long neck and jaws like spears. He looked like a dragon. His wingspan was thirty-three feet, and his feet had talons.

Just imagine what it looked like when a dozen Quetzalcoatlus pterosaurs flew over a lake. It looked like a dozen dragons were flying over that lake. If you've seen movies such as *Jurassic Park* or *Lost World,* you've seen Hollywood's view of the pterosaurs. Usually, the movie industry portrays the pteranodon, giving the species horrifying teeth when, in actuality, the flying dinosaur was toothless. Another interesting thing about the pterosaurs is that they did *not* have scales. Rather, they were leathery and furry. Not quite our image of a dragon, but close enough.

The pterosaurs swooped through the ancient sky for hours and hours before growing tired. Scientists believe that the pterosaurs had large birdlike brains and complex social behaviors. And like dragons, they hatched from eggs. The first pterosaur fossils we have date back to approximately 200 million years ago, and given that the giant Quetzalcoatlus were flapping around the planet 65 million years ago, these dragon creatures lived on Earth for (this is a hard math problem) approximately 135 million years. That's a really long time.

Even though humans didn't exist until, say, 3.5 million years ago, it still makes a lot of sense that humans all over the world believed in ancient dragons who lived for thousands of years.

In addition, it makes sense that early humans believed in dragons because they routinely encountered giant snakes and considered them to be serpent dragons. These serpent dragons had no wings or limbs, but they did sport dragon heads and horns, and they did have nasty-looking crocodile jaws. Modern examples of huge serpents include the rock python and the Indian python, each reaching lengths of thirty feet and weighing several hundred pounds. Considering that pythons have existed longer than humans, it's very possible that the early humans, who were much smaller than us in size, saw these giant pythons as killer dragons.

Other stories of dragon encounters may have been due to the presence of creatures who still live today, such as the Komodo Dragon, which is a huge lizard that populates five small Indonesian islands. The Komodo dragon attacks animals as large as deer and wild pigs, and sometimes it will attack a person.

As far as fantasy creatures go, dragons come in a wide variety of species and flavors, so many that you might think the creatures really existed. . . .

In the 1600s, scholars still wrote about dragons as real animals who lived long ago. They were not considered fantasy creatures by most people. For example, in 1608, a scientist named Edward Topsell wrote that dragons were reptiles who were closely related to serpents. Like many people, he believed that dragons were routinely seen and even killed by divers.[2]

---

2. Dr. Desmond Morris in a foreword to Karl Shuker, *Dragons: A Natural History* (London, England: Barnes & Noble Books, 1995) p. 8.

Dragons are known around the world. In Hawaii, dragons are called *kelekona,* and in China, they're called *lung.* The Cherokee Indians call them *unktena,* and the Fins know dragons as *lohikaarme.* Polish people tell stories about *smok,* the Japanese have dragon stories about *tatsu.* In Turkey, dragons are known as *ejderha,* in Welsh they're *draig,* and in Germany, they're *lindwurm.* The list is extensive.

Before the 1600s and Edward Topsell, people everywhere thought that they really saw dragons. For example, between the eleventh and thirteenth centuries in the British Isles, these and many other towns claimed to have battles with dragons: Uffington, Anwick, BenVair, Brinsop, Dornoch, Llanrhaedr-Ym-Mochant, Kirkton, Ludham, Carhmaptin, Penmynnedd, Denbigh, Bromfeld, Deerhurst, St. Osyth, Wantley, Bures, St. Leonard's Forest, Bisterne, and Alear.

Speaking of serpent dragons, most people have heard of the Loch Ness Monster, and there are lakes inhabited by reptile monsters all over the world, including in Norway and Japan. The Loch Ness monster, also known as Nessie, is a famous Scottish serpent dragon. According to folklore, the Loch Ness Monster dwells in a lake (called Loch Ness), and occasionally it rises in giant swells from the water, its undulating thirty-foot-long snakelike body dipping up and down across the surface. Nessie has a dragon's head and a very long neck. Actually the Loch Ness "lake" is a channel that is about 755 feet deep and twenty-three miles long. Rivers connect Loch Ness to the North Sea and the Atlantic Ocean.

Nessie was first seen in ancient times, way back in A.D. 690 or so, and people have seen her ever since. Still, there are no photographs of her, nor any serious proof that she exists.

But let's move beyond Scotland and take a look at dragons in other lands. In Greek mythology, Zeus encounters Typhon, demon of the whirlwind. Typhon is a monster made from coiled snakes with hundreds of serpent heads and huge, leathery wings. In addition, Typhon breathes fire, just like a dragon. Greek mythology also includes the hydra, a multiheaded dragon with deadly breath. And the Greeks also had Oroboros, a dragon with clawed feet.

One of the most famous Greek dragons is the ancient creature of the earth known as the Drakon, guardian of treasures and sacred springs. The Drakons were something of a clan, resembling gigantic serpents, having the wisdom of gods, and guarding their treasures at the expense of your life; that is, they would kill you should you trespass into their carefully protected sacred sites.

One Drakon, simply named Python, was a female dragon living beside a spring until Apollo, one of the ancient Greek gods, killed her with arrows. (How is it that in all the old legends dragons were killed with bows and arrows? I'd think it would take something a lot more powerful to do away with a gigantic beast who's survived since the dawn of time.)

Apollo created the Oracle at Delphi on the spot where he killed Python. For centuries, people reenacted the slaying of Python at the Delphi Oracle in honor of Apollo and the old Drakon.

But the story doesn't end there. Remember, I mentioned that the Drakons were something of a clan, meaning there was more than one of them. So, continuing the story of Python and Apollo and the Oracle at

Famous Dragons Who Aren't Really Dragons

"What's Lois talking about this time?" you may be wondering. How can a dragon not be a dragon?

Here are some clues:

- Des Moines Dragons, a basketball team
- Orlando Dragons, another basketball team
- Sonoma Sea Dragons, a swimming team
- Portland Forest Dragons, a football team
- San Antonio Dragons, a hockey team
- Bethesda Dragons, an "under-eleven" soccer team
- Battle Dragons, a paintball team
- Australia's St. George Dragons, a rugby team
- Brisbane's Dragon Volleyball Association, for volleyball enthusiasts.

Now you understand what I'm talking about! Dragons are popular choices when naming sports teams.

Delphi, a guy named Cadmus, founder of Thebes, asked the Oracle for guidance one day. The Oracle was a source of great wisdom, foretelling things to come and dispensing advice to all who asked for it. The Oracle gave Cadmus the following advice: go to a spring that's guarded by one of Python's buddies. Now, most people wouldn't go to a spring in search of a giant monster-dragon who's lived since the dawn of time, but Cadmus was brave and off he went.

He found the dragon. It had triple rows of teeth. Of course, it was huge and scary. Cadmus did not pull out a bow and arrow to kill this dragon. No, that would be too easy of a kill. Rather, Cadmus picked up a rock and smashed it on the dragon's head. (How did these guys *do* that? How did they kill dragons with a rock or with a bow and arrow? You tell me, because I haven't a clue!)

But the story still isn't done. There's more.

Cadmus whacked the dragon over the head with a rock. The dragon died. Cadmus made some sacrifices to the goddess Athena, who told him to plant the dragon's teeth (all three rows of them) in the soil as if they were seeds. Of course, Cadmus, who always obeyed oracles and goddesses and that sort of thing, immediately planted the teeth, and poof, all the teeth sprouted into warriors.

I hate to tell you, but the story continues even further. There are kings and golden fleeces and witches, and the story even contains a thousand-coiled dragon. I could fill many pages just telling you about the Drakons of Greece.

If you think about it, dear old Saphira is a pleasant gal compared to some of these dragons of old folklore. She doesn't have a thousand coils. She doesn't have three rows of horrific teeth. She doesn't lay in wait to kill anyone who comes near a particular fountain of water. And it seems to take a lot more than a little arrow to get rid of her. Something tells me she can't be beaten that easily. Certainly not with a rock.

Of course, the Romans also believed in dragons, and in fact, the Latin word *draco* is translated into "huge snakes and dragons." The Roman version also breathed fire and looked like a giant reptilian monster with wings.

In Scandinavian countries, dragons were everywhere. The Vikings had boats with dragon heads on them. In ancient legends, dragons were huge serpents with talons, a huge mouth housing sharp teeth and blowing fire, and a lashing tail. They hoarded treasures and killed people. And in Europe, people also believed in dragons that had twin heads and in griffins who looked like a cross between lions, birds, raptors, and reptiles.

In India, dragons were also everywhere. The creator god Vishnu was often shown half asleep on the back of a dragon-hydra, or *naga*. The shapeshifting Indian dragon, the *makara*, usually appeared as a monster with a snake tail and the head of a crocodile, or simply as a dragon or sea serpent.

Asian dragons caused floods, and references to them range back as far as 2700 B.C. Chinese dragons had claws, scales, and giant mouths with sharp teeth. In Japan, the Koshi dragon was so immense that its body could sit on eight hills and valleys at one time. It had a scaled back, eight tales, and eight heads. The Mongols believed in the *leongalli* dragon, who was half chicken and half lion.

In approximately 5000 B.C., stories described a Sumerian dragon named Zu. This dragon stole some tablets from Enlil, a god who enlisted the sun-god Ninurta to get the tablets back and kill Zu.

Often, sea monsters, aka dragons, fought gods, too. For example, Enuma Elish, which is an early Babylonian myth, spoke of the dragons Apsu (the name means "fresh water") and Tiamat (the name means "salt sea"). These two dragons begot the first gods and from them came all creatures. In the Canaanite Poem of Baal, a young god defeated the seven-headed sea dragon Yam-Nahar. An early Egyptian story told of the sea dragon Apophis trying to kill the Egyptian sun god Ra.

Let's return for a moment to the Babylonian dragon Tiamat, one of the most horrific and huge dragons throughout history. Before even the skies, heavens, and Earth were named, Tiamat was literally the salt water of the primal sea. Later, she became a dragon with a hide so thick that weapons could not puncture it. Apsu, the other Babylonian dragon, was all the fresh water of the world. He wasn't a dragon at first, either. It was only when the sea waters of Tiamat mingled with the fresh waters of Apsu that Tiamat became a female dragon and Apsu became a male dragon. In addition, their offspring, tiny dragonettes, were produced when the waters mingled.

The tiny dragonettes were hard to handle. Apsu wasn't a very nice father, and he decided to destroy his own children. Young gods didn't want Apsu to kill his own children, so they cast spells upon him and their magic destroyed Apsu. (Families in mythology tend to be extremely dysfunctional. If you think you have it bad because of some problems at home, imagine what it would be like to be the child of Apsu and Tiamat.)

Tiamat was pretty upset, to put it mildly, when her husband, dear old Apsu, was murdered by the gods. She decided to get even, so she sent monsters of all kinds to battle the gods. Her monsters included horned serpents, venom-bloated giant snakes, scorpion men, bull men, fish men, and even demons. Tiamet was one powerful dragon.

Who did the gods send to fight all these monsters? Marduk, their young god king. One guy. And what did Marduk bring with him to fight all these monsters?

Surely you can guess the answer by now: a bow, some arrows, and a huge net. *Of course.*

The net had to be *huge,* say, half the size of the planet. Remember, Tiamet was once all the sea water in the entire world. This was no mere fish net for catching tuna. I can't imagine how Marduk carried such a big net, much less how he tossed it over giant monsters.

But he did exactly that. After all, Marduk had special powers. He gathered the winds and rode a chariot on the storm to arrive at Tiamet's humble abode (which was probably an entire ocean). And then he captured Tiamet in the net and magically sent the wind into her face. She basically choked on the wind, and the wind filled her stomach so much that her belly bulged out like a marshmallow the size of New York City. Marduk simply stuck one arrow in his bow, and *ding*, shot the arrow into her heart. When Tiamet fell, all the demons and other monsters raced away (sissies!). Marduk—calm, cool, and collected—split Tiamet in half. I don't know what he used for this spectacular feat. Maybe he simply used magic and cast a spell upon

Tiamet to chop her into two pieces. He then clearly used magic to make half of her body the Earth, and the other half of Tiamet's body the sky. Finally, Marduk killed her monster buddy Kingu, and from Kingu's blood, Marduk created people.

There are few dragon stories that can equal the tale of Apsu and Tiamet. Of course, Tiamet already had children and relatives at the time she was slain by Marduk. It is said that one of her relatives is the rainbow serpent of South Africa. This serpent is huge (well, it is related to Tiamet, and she wasn't exactly petite), and it sleeps at the bottom of the ocean with its body wrapped around the entire planet.

In India and Ethiopia, dragons are also huge, though not the size of all the oceans on the planet. The Indian-Ethiopian dragon is 180 feet long and has a magic healing jewel between his eyes. If a human steals the jewel and wears it on his arm, he becomes invincible.

There's a black dragon who lives in the marshes, and there's also a golden dragon who flies and lives in the mountains. The golden dragon has scales, a beard, and a tail that's strong enough to kill with one lash. He lives in the bowels of the Earth, and when he's hungry he emerges from his den and hunts elephants.

Chinese dragons come in four main forms: Tien-Lung, the Celestial Dragon, who protects the places where gods live; Shen-Lung, the Spiritual Dragon, who controls rains and other storms; Ti-Lung, the Earth Dragon, who controls rivers; and Fut-Lung, the Under-world Dragon, who guards treasures.

Dragons of all kinds have been taken very seriously throughout Chinese history. Five-toed dragons were a symbol of great power and supposedly spoke directly to the gods. Only the Chinese Emperors were "allowed" to communicate with these five-toed Imperial Dragons, and the penalty to citizens of attempting discourse with a five-toed dragon was death.

It has been postulated that the ancient Chinese be-lief in dragons stemmed from the discovery of dinosaur bones. It is conceivable that giant creatures were un-earthed from their graves and that the ancient Chinese believed these creatures were dragons.

Taken collectively, the Chinese dragon is benevolent and controls the sea, sky, and earth. When provoked, the dragon might destroy a village or cause a huge storm, but when people act kindly and do not anger the dragon, he causes no harm and actually bestows blessings.

Not only does the dragon bring good fortune, he is the founder of royal families. His head is horselike and has horns. He has long whiskers, scales on his body, and four legs. He likes to play with a ball of light known as the sacred pearl. Somewhere, way up high in the clouds, a jade tablet lists all dragons and their numbers. These dragons came into being a very long time ago, and they evolved from water snakes into their ultimate, powerful dragon form. Chinese dragons, taken as a whole, are shapeshifters, and their leader is Lung, ruler of the sky.

Chinese people who believe in dragons disagree about what Lung looks like and exactly what he does. Some say he has deer horns on a camel's head. Some say he has ox ears and a snake's neck. Some say he has fish scales, tiger paws, and the belly of a clam. Rather than blowing fire, Lung blows clouds.

It is said that four main dragon kings live beneath

the ocean in shining palaces. From there, they rule the four oceans of the Earth. It is also said that the five-toed Imperial Dragon was responsible for the creation of the first Chinese Emperor, who had a dragon's tail.

Clearly, Saphira's ancestry is not that of a Chinese dragon. Nor is she as big and monstrous as Tiamet or Apsu. Rather, she resembles the stereotypical Western dragon: wings, fire breath, serpentine. Most Western dragons have crests on their heads and beards. They have bright eyes, just like Saphira's eyes; teeth, horns, scales, claws, large spiny wings, and long tails. A dragon with two legs is called a wyvern, but many dragons have four legs. And just like Saphira, they breathe fire and smoke.

It is said that the head of a Western dragon contains a dragon stone, which is a brilliant gem with healing powers. In addition, the dragon's blood can heal even the most serious wounds. If a human befriends a dragon and gets a small dose of dragon blood, the human can then communicate with all the beasts in nature, understanding what birds are saying, what toads like to do for fun, and that sort of thing. This blood myth is similar to what we read in *Eragon*, whereby Saphira

Famous Men and Their Dragons

Merlin is probably one of the most famous magicians of all time. When fortress walls were collapsing in North Wales, Merlin determined it was because two dragons were imprisoned beneath the fortress. So, Merlin gave the dragons their freedom and the walls stopped collapsing.

Beowulf was a famous Dutch king who had to fight a local dragon to save his people. Remember, some dragons like to hoard treasures, so this particular dragon became infuriated when one of the cups in his treasure stash disappeared. Beowulf fought the dragon and was not doing particularly well when his servant, Wiglaf, stabbed the dragon. Beowulf was then able to kill the dragon. (Poor dragon.)

In 2926 B.C., a man named Fu Hsi came across a dragon on the banks of the Yellow

River in China. The dragon taught Fu Hsi how to write, and then Fu Hsi taught other people how to write, as well as how to play music, tame animals, and do math.

Even Marco Polo, the Italian traveler you might remember from social studies class, believed in dragons. Marco Polo believed that he encountered numerous dragons during his travels, among them wyverns that hunted elephants.

breathes herself into Eragon by marking his palm with a special oval.

The famous biblical creature Leviathan of the Book of Job was probably a dragon. He breathed fire and had thick scales that were immune to weapons. It's possible that Leviathan was based on observations of a real sea creature called an oarfish. Oarfish are extremely rare and live in the deepest parts of the ocean. Slender and bright yellow, they have a raised dorsal fin on the tops of their heads and possibly the fin looks like a dragon crest. They *are* huge, growing up to sixty feet long. I kid you not: the oarfish is really that long.

Western dragons were not considered kind and wonderful as were the Chinese dragons. In the early days, people even thought that it might have been a dragon rather than a snake who gave Eve the apple.

The idea of the evil dragon probably arose from the early church notions that Saint George killed a monster-dragon and that the crusaders had to battle dragons to save our souls and our lives. As for Saint George, he battled his dragon in Libya in the town of Silene. This was way back in the fourth century. A huge dragon rose from the swamps outside of town. The dragon had enormous batlike wings, four legs, a long tail, and thick green armored scales. Foul gas spewed from its mouth, killing anyone who breathed the noxious fumes.

The townspeople tried to subdue the dragon by feeding it two sheep a day. But eventually, the town ran out of sheep.

The stupid king decided to sacrifice a child a day. The townspeople were entered in a lottery, whereby every day one unlucky mother drew her child's name and that poor child was fed to the dragon.

Weeks passed. The dragon kept eating all the children. In fact, finally, the king's own daughter was chosen by the lottery. The people tied her to a stake by the dragon's swamp.

Poor Aleyone, the daughter, thought she was doomed when the earth started shaking like crazy. She was sure it was the dragon. But it wasn't. Instead, it was Saint George. He wore silver armor with a big red cross on his breastplate. He even rode a white horse and carried a white shield.

Saint George untied princess Aleyone and then turned

his attention to the swamp where the dragon rose in a mighty tower of slime. The dragon spread his giant wings and roared. For a minute, George blinked at the shocking colors of the dragon's scales in the sunlight, but then he gathered his senses and thrust his sword into the monster's neck. (George must have been awfully tall to reach the monster's neck with his sword.) The dragon was almost dead at this point, so Saint George and the princess dragged the poor thing back to Silene where George beheaded it in front of all the townspeople. (I wonder how a child princess and one young man dragged a gigantic monster back to town, but I am willing to suspend disbelief whenever I read dragon stories and other folktales.)

As mentioned earlier in this book, it's common for dragon novels to use Dragon Riders, humans who are close friends with the dragons and who communicate with the dragons through mental telepathy. Even Eragon's saddle has been seen before: take a look (a very detailed and long look) at the section called "Taming and Flying Dragons" in *Dragonology: The Complete Book of Dragons* by Dr. Ernest Drake. In this beautiful and fascinating book, you'll see a large illustration of a man riding his dragon using a saddle. Further, you'll be instructed that, should you want to be a Dragon Rider, it would be wise to "keep a firm hold on the reins."[3] In addition, the book supplies details about how dragons dive and swoop and how you can learn to ride a dragon using various sophisticated techniques.

In the case of *Eragon,* we're told that dragons have more than one type of saddle. Brom and Eragon make a simple saddle for Saphira using five bands of leather, long leather cords, and padding. The book contains a detailed explanation of how Brom and Eragon construct the saddle, and this part of the book is fascinating. Saphira's saddle includes a loop that sits over her neck spikes, and it has comfortable, loose bands between her front legs.

Unlike most dragons of real folklore, Saphira is witty and often says very wise and mature things to Eragon, such as "This is irritating, having to hide all the time like a criminal."[4] Reading all of her witticisms and

3. Dr. Ernest Drake, *Dragonology: The Complete Book of Dragons* (Cambridge, Massachusetts: Candlewick Press).
4. *Eragon,* pp. 129–130.

intelligent analyses, I was wondering if dragons are hatched with mature, adult intelligence. How do they learn language and such complex adult ways of thinking while they're in the egg for hundreds of years? When using mental telepathy, are they using English to "talk" to their humans?

While they don't appear in *Eragon* or *Eldest,* there's one more type of dragon I'd like to mention. These are hybrid dragons, part other animal and part dragon. I'm mentioning them because they would be interesting additions to the *Eragon* trilogy or to any fantasy book. In fact, you may want to use these dragon-beasts later in this book when you will attempt to write your own fantasy story.

Yes, did you catch the word "dragon-beast" in my last sentence? There are dragon-beasts in the *Eragon* trilogy, but they are simply smaller versions of dragons. They aren't hybrid creatures such as the ones in real folklore. For example, in folklore, we have dragon-carps, which have dragon heads and gigantic carp bodies with gigantic carp tails. The dragon-carp can talk to humans. We also have dragon-tigers (I'm not joking—would I kid around with you?), which have tiger heads and dragon bodies. There are dragon-wolves, with—take a big guess!—wolf heads and dragon bodies. And on and on . . .

What would be the strangest hybrid of all? You tell me.

· 4 ·
Dwarves, the Shade, Urgals, Giants, and Other Beasties

Other than Eragon, Brom, Arya, Saphira, and other main characters, some of the most interesting characters in *Eragon* and *Eldest* are the dwarves, giants, Urgals, white raven, and of course, the Shade. It might seem odd to someone who hasn't read *Eragon* and *Eldest* that I would mention so many characters. But to those of us who have read the books, it seems the opposite, that perhaps

I'm naming only a small percentage of all the characters.[1]

Among other creatures, this chapter talks about the dwarves. What are they like in *Eragon* and *Eldest,* and what are they like in traditional folklore? How similar are the novels to the traditional stories? Along the way, we'll also discuss the Shade and Urgals, the giants, and a few other beasties.

First, let's start with the dwarves.

For thousands of years, Dragon Riders protected the planet and the dwarves were their friends. According to Brom, the dwarves, along with the dragons, are the "true inhabitants" of the world. The dwarves lived in Alagaësia even before the elves traveled there by sea on silver ships. But after the Dragon Riders were destroyed, people lost track of what happened to the dwarves.[2] Later, in the first novel, Eragon lands in the dwarves' capital, Tronjheim, where he learns that

---

1. Just for fun, I'll name some more characters: Katrina, Uncle Garrow, Horst, Albriech, Baldor, Roran, Marian, Ismira, Selena, Galbatorix, Morzan, Gertrude, Trianna, Angela, Gannel, Islanzadi, Blagden, Orik, Glaedr, Oromis. Which ones (or hundreds!) did I miss?
2. Paolini, *Eragon,* pp. 49–51.

the dwarves, elves, and Varden have all agreed that new Dragon Riders must be trained by Brom and then by the elves. Eragon meets Hrothgar, the dwarf king, and various other court dwarves, and battles take place in the dwarves' tunnels.

The dwarves are prominent throughout the second book, *Eldest*. We learn that they usually live underground, though sometimes they prefer to live in cities, such as the dwarf city called Tarnag. We also learn that dwarves are tiny, that their doorways are less than five feet tall, and that they have an elaborate creation story.

A creation story, which we'll discuss more in a minute, is how a group of people describe their beginnings. In real life, there are many hundreds, maybe thousands, of different creation stories from all over the world. Most involve gods, monsters, giants, and other fantastic creatures.

In the case of the *Eragon* and *Eldest* dwarves, the creation story has to do with a she-wolf, statues and burnt offerings, the King of Gods named Guntera, the Goddess of Rivers and Seas named Kilk, and many other gods. Helzvog owns the hearts of all dwarves because he formed the first dwarf from the roots of mountains after the giants disappeared from the world. It was only after the dwarves and elves were created that people arose from the soil.

In the real world, how do we view dwarves? Do they really live in tunnels in our folk stories? Do they manipulate elements and metals, as they do in *Eragon* and *Eldest*? Are they small, do they perform magic, are they kind or evil, do they have elaborate creation myths?

In our chapter about elves, we talked a little about fairies. An elf is a type of fairy according to most folklore. The same can be said about dwarves—they are another type of fairy. Most of the world's people have ancient stories relating to dwarves.

Dwarves usually have long, gray beards and look really old. They are miners who live in tunnels, according to legends, so their role in *Eldest* conforms to what we know in reality about dwarves. Now why do they live in tunnels? And in real folklore, why do they *not* live in cities, as they sometimes do in the world of *Eragon*? Ancient stories say that dwarves are toads during the day. If the dwarves are hit by sunlight, they turn to stone. This would be good reason not to leave the tunnels, don't you think?

Dwarves are small and they look like misshaped humans. According to folklore, dwarves turn metal into beautiful but dangerous artifacts. These artifacts possess spells and curses. The dwarves are often invisible because they wear magic clothing. As with the dwarves in *Eragon* and *Eldest,* our "real" dwarves are magical, and if you remember the giant sapphire that the dwarves worship, it seems apparent that the *Eragon* dwarves also possess beautiful and magical artifacts.

As you might have guessed, there are many types of dwarves in the real world, and overall, they are considered to be a type of goblin. On the island of Rugen in the Baltic Sea, people identify three types of dwarves, solely based on the color of their clothes—white, brown, or black.

The white dwarves are kind and gentle, and they spend their time mining gold and silver from underground caverns. In the summer, they dance in the form of butterflies. While the *Eragon* and *Eldest* dwarves don't dance in the form of butterflies, they do seem kind and gentle for the most part, and they do spend most of their time in those underground tunnels digging for precious minerals. It seems very likely that Christopher Paolini's dwarves are white ones.

Brown dwarves are mischievous and cause a lot of trouble. They also steal babies, which is extremely bad behavior. I don't think Paolini's dwarves are of the brown variety.

Then there are the black dwarves of our real folklore. These black dwarves are pure evil. They're ugly, too. (Have you ever wondered why all the evil magical beings are ugly, while the nice magical beings are beautiful or handsome? Why can't we have a beautiful yet evil black dwarf, or an ugly yet kindhearted nymph?) The black dwarves use false lights to lure treasure-laden ships to shore, then the dwarves attack the ships and steal all the treasures. They make deadly weapons out of ore that they mine, which is a lot worse than making artifacts that cast spells. When not killing and stealing, the black dwarves turn into owls that screech constantly. Well, clearly, Christopher Paolini's dwarves are not of the black variety!

The standard dwarf creation story of our world differs substantially from the dwarf creation story of *Eragon*. A very well-known dwarf creation story comes from Iceland and Scandinavia. In this story, dwarves end up holding the entire world in place.

The Norse people, or Vikings, recorded their beliefs in what is called the Younger Edda, written by Snorri Sturluson in approximately 1220. Sturluson based his Younger Edda on the oral (spoken) myths of the Elder or Poetic Edda. In this story, the world was created from the body of the Evil Ice Giant, Ymir.

As the story goes, King Gylfi, who ruled what we now call Sweden, learned about the Aesir, the gods from Valhalla. Gylfi disguised himself and went to Valhalla to meet the High One and learn all about Aesir and the beginning of the world.

The High One explained that there were two atmospheres, one in the north, the other in the south. The northern atmosphere was dark and icy; the southern was light and warm. Between the two atmospheres was total emptiness, called Ginnungagap. Within the void of Ginnungagap, the cold northern air mingled with the warm southern air, creating moisture, and hence, life began to form. The first form of life was the Evil Ice Giant called Ymir.

Ymir was alone in Ginnungagap, but he lay down, and while resting, his armpits gave birth to a man and a woman, and his legs mated to create a son. A family of ogres was born. As the ice melted in Ginnungagap, it turned into a cow giant named Auohumla, whose milk turned into nutritious rivers. A man arose from some ice that Auohumla was licking, and he was Buri the Strong, whose son Bor married Bestla, a daughter of the original ogres. Bor and Bestla had a child, the great god Odin, as well as other children, the gods Vili and Ve. These gods rose up and killed Ymir, the Evil Ice Giant, and then took the giant's corpse to the middle of Ginnungagap, where they transformed his blood into the oceans and his body into the earth. Mountains formed from his bone; and rocks from his teeth. His brains became the clouds. Ymir's skull became the top of the sky and was held up in the north, south, east, and west by four dwarves.

The Scandinavians say that the dwarves were created

by maggots that crawled from Ymir's body and that there are three types of dwarves. The first is a group called Modsognir's folk, the second is Durin's group, and the third is known as Dwalin's alliance with Lovar. The dwarves make magic spears, ships, and other objects—even magic hair.

In standard Norse folklore, dwarves lived in caves located in Nideavellir. They made magic items such as Thor's hammer, which always returned to his hand after he threw it or lost it. They also made a boar with golden bristles who was named Gullinbursti and could travel anywhere on the land, in the air, or through the sea. They made magic rings, including Draupnir, a golden armband that produced eight more magic armbands on every ninth night.

The dwarves in Tolkien's *Lord of the Rings* are very similar to the dwarves in standard mythology, as well as in *Eragon* and *Eldest*. In fact, drawing heavily on folklore, Tolkien's work provided the basis for much of modern fantasy tales, including *Eragon* and *Eldest*. In the *Lord of the Rings*, the dwarves in Middle Earth toiled endlessly with precious metals from which they made magical items. They lived inside mountains and caverns, and they dug for metal in tunnels. They looked like standard dwarves with long beards and short heights. Though pleasant and musical, the dwarves could fight with the best of 'em when necessary.

The dwarves who befriend Eragon share some pretty obvious traits with Tolkien's dwarves, who in turn follow the standard folklore patterns. What about the trolls and giants? Well, these fantasy creatures are mentioned in passing in *Eragon* and *Eldest,* but they don't play very large roles—not yet, anyway.

Very early in *Eldest,* the Urgals attack some trolls and kill them. These trolls may come into play more in the third novel, which isn't available at the time that I'm writing this book. But as *Eldest* closes, we know very little about the trolls.

In real folklore, trolls have many different names. Around the world, they are known as berg people, jutul, tusse, hill men, and trows, among others. Belief in trolls began in Germany and Scandinavia, but troll stories are found everywhere. Supposedly, trolls guard bridges and byways. They don't guard these places for good reasons, either. Usually, trolls hide beneath the bridges, then jump out and scare people half to death, demanding huge amounts of money and treasure, sometimes even human life.

In the real world, the Scandinavian people believe that trolls are giants and that the biggest troll is their king, Dovregubben, who lives in the Dovre mountain. Trolls have rough hair and mossy growths on their heads, and they supposedly stir soup with their long noses.

Trolls live a long time, just like other creatures of Fairy Land, but sunlight turns trolls into stone. You might remember from our earlier discussion that sunlight also turns dwarves into stone. Some trolls have multiple heads, and some only have one eye, which sits in the middle of their foreheads.

As for the giants in *Eragon* and *Eldest,* they supposedly lived long ago but disappeared, so we don't know much about them, either. Giants, of course, have been featured in fantasy stories for as long as people have been telling fantasy stories. In Greek mythology, for example, the giants called Titans governed all the main parts of the planet. They were the children of Mother

Earth and the Heavenly Sky. Mother Earth also had other gigantic children, such as the one-eyed giant Cyclops as well as giants with one hundred arms and fifty heads. The giant Antaeus built a temple made from skulls, and as long as Antaeus's feet touched the earth, nobody could kill him. So along came Hercules, who lifted the giant and then strangled him.

In Norse mythology, rock and frost giants battled gods from their giant homes in Jotunheim. Giants who wanted to destroy the world fought the gods in Ragnarok. Of all the gods that the giants hated, the thunder god Thor was the most despised. Remember, he was the god with the hammer made by the dwarves.

Returning to *Eragon* and *Eldest,* it's possible that the giants who were on the land at the beginning of time were patterned after the giants in the book of Genesis in the Bible. According to the Bible, giants roamed the Earth in long ago days, and Goliath, possibly the most famous giant, was killed by David.

Now, what about the Shade? Who or what is he in *Eragon*? Is he a giant, a troll, a dwarf, an elf, a dragon, or something else?

Here's what we know about him from the novels:

The Shade is able to perform amazing magic, such as muttering something and then burning down forests simply by lifting his hand. In fact, by yelling "Garjzla!," the Shade shoots fire balls from his palms, something we often see in cartoons such as Dragonball Z. He's able to transport things from one place to another, an ability we'll discuss in chapter 5, "Magic: How Do They *Do* That?" On the first page of Eragon, we're told that the Shade is very tall and looks like a human, except that he has maroon eyes (not exactly a natural human eye color). He has bright red hair and he's in cahoots with the nasty Urgals.

Speaking of Urgals, they're defined right away in *Eragon,* too, on page 1. Paolini tells us that they look like men with huge, muscular arms and bowed legs. They're made for fighting, their blood is black, and horns grow above their ears. The Urgals are totally evil, and a good time for them is destroying entire villages and killing everyone they encounter.

And speaking of Urgals and the Shade, he's not

always nice to them. On page 5 of *Eragon*, the Shade shoots fire at the Urgals and kills them.

Long ago, Galbatorix hung out with another Shade, as apparently there are a few of these Shade characters, and this particular one used black magic to cause a Dragon Rider to revolt. This was the beginning of all sorts of trouble leading up to Eragon's time.

The final *Eragon* creature that's worth noting is the white raven who first appears on page 227. His name is Blagden and he cackles things that are clearly intended to be a play on Edgar Allan Poe's raven in his most famous poem. For example, Blagden says, "And on the door was graven evermore . . ." and so forth, which is a clear reference to Poe's poem.

It was Blagden who saved the life of Arya's father during a fight with an Urgal. The raven pecked out the Urgal's eyes in the nick of time. The elf father was so grateful that he bestowed magical powers upon Blagden. That magic cost Blagden the color in his feathers.

So, who is Edgar Allan Poe and what about his "evermore" raven? Well, Poe was an extremely famous author who wrote dark stories and poems in the early

1800s. He died in 1849. His most famous poem is probably "The Raven." Some of his other stories and poems were "The Purloined Letter," "The Tell-Tale Heart," and "The Murders in the Rue Morgue," which may be the first modern detective story ever penned.

In "The Raven," which Poe wrote in 1845, someone is whispering the name Lenore on a very spooky night. There's a tapping on the window, and the man telling us the story flings open the shutter to find a raven perched on the sill. The raven says one word to the man: "Nevermore." The man cannot fathom what the raven means by the word.

Basically, what happens in the poem is that a lonely guy is miserable because he has lost his love, Lenore, and a raven shows up to murmur Lenore's name and croak one word, nevermore. The man assumes that the bird is croaking nevermore not through wisdom, but only because some clever master has taught him to say it. Realizing that the raven will answer nevermore to every question, the man poses questions such as "Is there balm in Gilead?" and "Can Lenore be found in paradise?" Finally, the man gives up, tells the bird to take "thy form from off my door," and sinks back into the shadow left by the raven upon the floor. The man's soul will never rise from that shadow. Nevermore.

When Blagden references the door and evermore, he's actually speaking in a way that directly references Poe's raven. And while it's interesting to note the use of the raven in the novels, it's also interesting to note the touches of real folklore in the forms of trolls, giants, and even wraiths, creatures who are mentioned but who basically don't appear in the books. Aside from the dragons and elves, the most prominent fantasy creatures in *Eragon* and *Eldest* seem to be the dwarves.

Disney's Seven Dwarves

Everyone probably remembers the story of *Snow White and the Seven Dwarfs* from Walt Disney, originally filmed in 1937. In the film, an evil queen wants to dispose of her beautiful stepdaughter, Snow White.

Who has a name like Snow White? Can you imagine how weird it would be if a new kid came to your school and her name was Snow White?

Because the queen is so mean, Snow White runs off and hides with seven dwarves in the forest. Then the queen turns into a witch and tricks Snow White into eating a poisoned apple.

I am reminded of all those apples that parents put into my trick-or-treat bag when I was a kid. My friends and I hated those apples, and we didn't think much of people who gave us apples on Halloween. Then, adult paranoia set in, probably with good cause, and it became almost a crime to give apples on Halloween. What if the apples were poisoned? Now, I wasn't born in 1937—no, I'm not *that* old, not yet—so I doubt the poisoned apple paranoia came from the 1937 movie version of *Snow White*.

Anyway, Snow White eats the apple and falls into a deep sleep from which she cannot awaken unless . . .

A handsome prince kisses her.

Of course, Prince Charming comes along, finds her in the glass coffin, kisses her, and she awakens to a life of everlasting perfection and happiness.

It is a fairy tale. In real life, I do not recommend that you eat a poison apple and pass out. The chances are very high— like 99.99999999999 percent high (like impossible)—that a handsome prince will *not* come along and kiss you, hence purging your body and brain of zombie poisons.

Actually, Walt Disney didn't come up with the original fairy tale. As with Christopher Paolini's dwarves, Disney's dwarves and his Snow White story were based on real and very old folk stories. In the case of Snow White, it's sometimes thought that Charles Perrault, who lived between 1628 and 1703, made up the original story. Scholars also think that Perrault made up other fairy tales, such as "Little Red Riding Hood," "Sleeping Beauty," and "Cinderella."[3] Of course, The Grimm Brothers, who are extremely famous folktale authors, are often credited with the creation of Snow White. The Grimms published a large collection of fairy tales in the early nineteenth century.

But back to Snow White and her seven dwarves. Do you remember their names?

Think for a minute.

Think, think, think.

---

3. http://www.penguinreaders.com/downloads/058242870X.pdf.

Take your time.

Now, if you answered "none of the dwarves had names," then I'm very impressed with your knowledge of folk tales. The original dwarves had no names. Good job!

Like most of us, though, you probably are trying to come up with the names of the seven dwarves who starred in the Walt Disney film. Here's the list I came up with: Dopey, Happy, Squeezy, Goofy, Silly, Sleazy, and Dufus-Head. I didn't do very well with this question.

Hopefully, you did better.

These are the names of Disney's seven dwarves: Bashful, Doc, Dopey, Grumpy, Happy, Sleepy, and Sneezy.

As a final note, here are their names in a few other languages:[4]

---

4. Derived from information at http://home.swipnet.se/%7Ew10744/disneyaniae/ dwarfnames.htm (a Web page that is no longer active as this book goes to press) and the Disney Comics mailing list quoted on the Web page (Volume 98, Issue #275 and Volume 98, Issue #281). The Web page lists many more languages and names. I just chose my favorites to share with you.

Bashful: Pimpel (German), Flovmand (Danish), Mammolo (Italian)

Doc: Chef (German), Brille (Danish), Kloker (Swedish)

Dopey: Dumpe (Danish), Dunga (Portuguese), Cucciolo (Italian), Kuka (Hungarian)

Grumpy: Gnavpot (Danish), Butter (Swedish), Sinnataggen (Norwegian), Brontolo (Italian), Grincheux (French)

Happy: Glucklich (German), Gongolo (Italian)

Sleepy: Schlafmutz (German)

Sneezy: Atchoum (French), Nuhanena (Finnish)

· 5 ·
Magic:
How Do They Do That?

In the last chapter, we briefly mentioned the Shade's use of magic, how he was able to mutter something to burn down a huge section of forest, and how he was able to mutter something else to instantly transport an object from one place to another. But there are many other examples of magic in *Eragon* and *Eldest*.

For example, on page 4 of *Eragon*, a female elf raises a sapphire stone over her head, utters magic words, and *poof*, the stone disappears as emerald color fills the forest.

She has teleported, or transported, the stone from one place to another.

When Galbatorix's dragon was killed, he went mad and wandered through the Spine, knowing he could hunt with magic. We're not told exactly how he would hunt using magic, nor are we told exactly what kinds of dark magic he learned from the Shade who helped him turn a Dragon Rider against the other Riders. We do know that Brom teaches Eragon how to kill game using elven language.[1]

The elves, of course, possess very strong magical skills. Brom tells Eragon that the elves use a powerful, secret language as the basis for much magic. This language "describes the true nature of things, not the superficial aspects that everyone sees," Brom explains.[2] By speaking the words that define the elemental natures of things, a person (or elf or dragon) can cause fire, water, floods, even teleportation. In fact, by speaking someone's true but hidden name, a being with

---

1. Paolini, *Eragon*, page 170.
2. Ibid., page 140.

magical power can make the person go mad. If the person doesn't go insane knowing his own inner name, he can gain enormous power over his own impulses.

In our own world, magic has always been feared by most people and is associated with witches and other demonic creatures. Angela the herbalist could be considered a witch. She uses herbs and magic potions, spells, and sorcery. She can foretell the future and uses crystal balls and tarot cards as well as other forms of magic.

In our world, a witch is somebody who is highly skilled at sorcery and other magical arts. The term "witch" comes from the Middle English *witche,* which comes from the Old English terms *wicca, wicce,* and *wiccian.* The "wicca" terms imply that the person works sorcery. Today's witches often claim to be practicing the wicca religion.

Witches use rituals, spells, herbs, hares, toads, and charms to manipulate nature, people, and inanimate objects. They talk to the spirits, they can be invisible, they can change shape, and they can heal simply by touching the person or animal that is injured. Although witches can be male, most of us think of witches as female.

Throughout history, people have feared and hated witches, thinking of them as old, mean-spirited hags who cast evil spells. The ancient Assyrians believed in sorcerers, witches, and wizards. The ancient Greek and Roman civilizations held that witches had special supernatural and magical powers, including great skill with herbs and potions. Witches in Rome brought the moon out of the sky, people thought; today, this is known as "drawing down the moon." As early as ancient Rome, people believed that witches worked with magic circles, made love potions (called Philtres), and called upon help from the spirits of the dead. Witches had the Evil Eye, which supposedly killed people by looking at them; a more rigorous definition of the Evil Eye is that it works even if the witch just thinks about doing evil.

In addition to magic circles, drawing down the moon, flying brooms, invisibility, shapeshifting, rituals, spells, herbs, love potions, and calling upon the dead for help, witches use familiars: small animals or spirits who keep them company and help them with their evil deeds. Angela's familiar is her werecat, Solembum.

Between 1450 and 1800, the Europeans hunted, tortured, and killed witches. This was a period of massive hatred and debauchery. Hideous cruelty was justified by church-loving people who thought witches ate people, sucked the blood from humans, and had sex with devils. Witches included jugglers, magicians, soothsaying wizards, enchanters, and charmers.

Witch mania swept the European continent and entered the United States where the infamous Salem witch trials condemned countless women and girls to their deaths. Their killers identified them as witches by identifying various signs, including not crying, a mole anywhere on the body, ugliness, a lumpy body, physical or mental handicaps, poverty, a bad temper. If a women or girl wasn't very well liked by her classmates or the townspeople, she might be considered to be a witch; as such, she was tortured to death, then hung and burned. To elicit confessions from witches, families were tortured in front of the accused.

In other cultures, witches are also considered to be evil. The Navajo think that witches are greedy men and women who hurt other people due to jealousy. To become a witch, the Navajo believe that a person must commit murder, rob graves, eat corpses, hold midnight sabbats, and make people sick.

We've all heard about covens, and it's pretty common knowledge that witches have leaders. In 1324, Alice Kyteler of Kilkenny, Ireland, was accused of being part of a thirteen-witch coven. During the Middle Ages, witches were tortured until they admitted they were in covens. The covens were secret organizations that did horrible things. In 1662, the Scottish witch Isobel Gowdie told her inquisitors that the witches were organized in covines, which were like squads.

Today, many witches claim to belong to covens that have existed for many hundreds of years. The witches say that they are descendants of generations of unbroken lines of witches and wizards. For example, Sybil Leek's New Forest coven supposedly has existed for eight hundred years.

Usually, a coven has twelve members plus one male

leader, who, according to witch hunters, is the devil or one of the devil's human representatives. During the Salem witch trials, testimony indicated that each coven had a summoner to tell the others about the next sabbat meeting; and a maiden, a young, beautiful girl who was the leader's escort at the sabbats.

Today's coven is a bit different from what I've just described. Typically, a modern coven meets at a sabbat, or circle, during the full moon. It also meets for eight seasonal festivals. The coven has a temple where it meets, and the witches tend to convene in the middle of a circle that extends three miles in each direction. Member witches are supposed to live within that three-mile zone. It's unlikely that in modern times these rules are observed in a strict fashion.

And, in today's coven, there is no male devil in charge escorted by his beautiful, young maiden. Instead, the modern coven tends to have a high priestess who represents the witch Goddess. If a male priest is in the coven, the female priestess, or Goddess, still rules as the top authority. If a maiden is present, she's an administrative assistant rather than an erotic escort.

The high priestess teaches magic to the other witches, purifies the coven's magic circle, and communicates with the supreme witch Goddess. She is in command of the spirits and the elements, and she directs all of the main rituals, chants, and magic of the coven. In general, there are no witch queens.

The Goddess is also known as Mother Nature or the Great Mother. She has infinite fertility and is responsible for bringing forth all life in the world. She creates and destroys, she controls the elements, and she is the moon, which, to witches, is the source of magical power. The Goddess is the font of psychic ability and intuition. People have been worshipping the Goddess since Paliolithic times. The earliest religions prayed and made sacrifices to Mother Earth, calling her by thousands of different names. Creation theories claimed that the Goddess was a female who self fertilized and gave rise to all beings. Many early societies had female leaders: they were matriarchal rather than patriarchal.

If you've been to a museum, you've seen the sculptures of females with the reproductive aspects exaggerated. These sculptures were probably made by ancient cultures to represent Mother Earth, or the Goddess. The Cro-Magnons in the Upper Paleolithic period (between 35,000 and 10,000 B.C.) made these pagan, female Goddess sculptures, often called "Venus figures." The Cro-Magnons drew pictures of childbirth on their cave walls. The Venus figure of Laussel, carved in approximately 19,000 B.C. in southern France, is painted red, and scholars suggest that the red connotes the blood of childbirth. In 4500 to 3500 B.C., people were still worshiping Venus figures, and in Africa in 7000 to 6000 B.C., the Horned Goddess, a self-fertilizing bisexual spiritual creature, was carved into cave walls. Ancient Egypt had its Goddess as well, in the form of Ta-Urt, the Great One, who was a pregnant hippopotamus. In 4000 B.C., Sumeria's queen and princesses were associated with the Goddess, while its king and princes were associated with God.

Between 1800 and 1500 B.C., when Abraham lived in Canaan, the worship of the Goddess began to decline. Later the church denounced pagan cults and religions that were based on the Goddess, as well. During the Middle Ages, the pagan Goddess called Diana was flourishing, and the church repressed worship of Diana as worship of a pagan diety.

Diana was a Goddess of the moon and remains one of the most significant aspects of modern witchcraft. She's a feminist Goddess, emphasizing independence, self-esteem, aggressive behavior, and positive attributes associated with worship of the moon. She is the modern patron Goddess of all witches.

Today's Goddess is closely associated with Gaia, the living consciousness of Earth, named after the Greek Goddess of Earth whose name was Gaia. Of course, the Shade, the elves, and Eragon use the ancient, hidden, "magic" words to connect to the elemental forces of the world: earth, air, water, and fire.

Clearly, life on Earth influences the planet in many ways. Each life-form affects the others; animals impact plants and vice versa; the environment is directly affected by what creatures do here on Earth. The planet supports a complex web of life and inanimate objects: rocks, clouds, the air, all are intertwined with humans, animals, and plants in a complex feedback system.

We've mentioned the word "elements" several times.

These elements—earth, air, water, and fire—are central to witchcraft and are aligned with the four points of the magic circle. They are also closely aligned with spirits know as elementals, which we discussed earlier in the chapter about elves. The earth elementals, including the elves and dwarves, are called gnomes. The air elementals are called sylphs, the water elementals are undines, and the fire elementals are salamanders.

Some elementals are created by witches simply by thinking; these elementals perform deeds and then disappear. It's as if "real" witches are collecting and condensing dust to do their will. Other elementals are found in nature in the form of spirits bound to animals, rocks, insects, plants, and so forth.

The elements themselves are derived from ancient beliefs, such as the categories of all beings devised by Plato: earth and pedestrians; air and birds; water and fish; and fire and stars. Occultists believe they must rule all the elements before mastering the spiritual realm.

The witches' familiars, such as Angela's werecat, are sources of elemental energy, and the witches bless their ritual tools with the four elements. Even the magic circle is consecrated using the four elements. The center binding all elements is the connection between the witches and the cosmic consciousness. As with Gaia, the witch circles and the beliefs about the elements—everything is alive in nature and rooted by a cosmic consciousness—pervades human mythology and folklore. It is the basis for elf magic in *Eragon* and *Eldest,* as well as in many other fantasy novels.

A witch circle represents a boundary in which concentrated magical power presides. The circle is a gateway to the gods, or to cosmic consciousness, and symbolizes the wholeness of the universe.

In ancient times, witches drew circles around sick people and newborn babies to protect them from the devil. Pagan stone circles are still found throughout England.

Witches must follow specific instructions when creating their circles. The circle must be drawn only during a particular time of day, and only if astrological conditions permit. A consecrated tool must be used. Before drawing a circle on it, a floor must be thoroughly scrubbed, and sometimes the witches sprinkle salt to define where the perimeter will be located. Most circles are nine feet in diameter. When drawing the circle, the head witch moves clockwise to represent the movement of the moon and other cosmic entities in the sky; to create a circle for negative magic, the witch moves counterclockwise. At this point, the witch consecrates the circle using the four elements, and she asks the spirits to protect the circle from demons.

The north quarter of the circle is associated with great power, darkness, and mystery. Because pagans often built their temples facing the North Star, the north became associated with the Christian Devil. Northern doors in ancient European churches are often called "the Devil's door." Christian ceremonies are rarely held on the northern sides of churches.

The south quarter of the circle is associated with the channeling of energy created by nature and psychic will. This area of the circle represents the sun, the element of fire, and the magic wand.

The east quarter represents illumination and enlightenment; it is associated with the sword and the element of air. The altar usually faces east, and quite often witches think that spiritual consciousness resides mainly in this quarter.

The final quarter, the west, represents fertility and emotions. It's associated with the chalice.

The altar, often placed inside the circle, is where the witches make offerings and hold ceremonies. It is associated with the Goddess, Gaia, or Mother Earth. Few requirements, oddly enough, are mandated when constructing the altar. One rule is that iron and steel should not be used, as these metals interfere with the magic energies created by ritual tools made from metal.

On the altar, the witches place various objects of worship. The black-handled, double-edged, six-inch athame knife directs energy and represents the element of fire. As a main ritual tool, it is used to carve or draw the magic circle and invoke and release the powers within the quarters. It is rarely used to cut anything other than a tiny doorway in the circle so people can pass into the circle; or a ritual cake, bread, or cord. The white-handled, double-edged, six-inch bolline (or boleen) knife is used to cut magical items such as herbs and to carve runes. The sword, like the althame, represents the element of fire. The peyton is a disk with a pentacle on its face. Its place is at the center of the altar, where it represents the female aspect of life. The wand represents the element of air and may be used in place of the althame to draw the circle and invoke the quarters. Of course, the magic wand is used when casting spells. The staff, a long version of the wand, is used to direct energy. The labrys, or double-headed axe, is also used to direct energy. Also on the altar are various crystals, oils, salt, water, wine, and bells, as well as statues and images of the gods. A thurible, or incense burner, is also located on the altar, and the incense purifies the air within the sacred space. Cauldrons and brooms are placed next to the altar in convenient locations should they be needed during the magical ceremonies.

The Book of Shadows is a modern tome that ancient witches didn't use. In the book are all the herbal remedies, spells, chants, dances, rules, rituals, and other material related to witchcraft. There is no one *Book of Shadows* corresponding to a witches' bible. Indeed, each coven may have its own *Book of Shadows.* You can think of the *Book of Shadows* as containing all those "hidden" words of magical power referenced by the elves in *Eragon* and *Eldest*.

As for spells, "drawing down the moon" is one of the most important modern rituals. In this ritual, a coven's high priestess becomes the Goddess and then utters spiritual poetry and other beautiful chants. The spells themselves are the words required to make something happen. They are also known as incantations, chants, charms, and runes. The rituals are actions that must be performed in a specific order while the witch utters the spells.

In *Eldest*, Oromis asks Eragon to define the word "magic." Eragon replies that magic is "the manipulation of energy through the use of ancient language."[3] This is completely in line with how magic is viewed in our world and in nearly all fantasy books. Of course, true to the spirit of magic teachers everywhere, Oromis adds that magic is more than the abra cadabra of incantations. It also has to do with the magical powers of the

---

3. Paolini, *Eldest*, page 354.

spellcasters. Again, this conforms directly to the spells of "real" witches and sorcerers throughout the ages.

Along with witches and their books of spells, their chants, and their rituals, the world's folklore is full of other examples of magic, ancient, "secret" languages. For example, an elaborate and very detailed book called the *I Ching* describes a language for foretelling the future and communicating with the basic elements of life. It's also called *The Book of Changes* or the *Chou I,* and it was developed in China a long time ago. The *I Ching* was studied by the Confucians during the last period of the Chou era, and was one of the few books that the Chinese government authorized. In 140 B.C., all non-Confucian texts were excluded from the imperial academy, making the *I Ching* doctrine. And, in fact, the imperial academy established a chair of study for the *I Ching,* which has lasted throughout Chinese history.

Over time, *The Book of Changes* or *I Ching* rose to a level far beyond that of a scholarly text. According to authorities on the *I Ching,* it came to be considered a volume of "sacred scriptures inspired by divine revelation.

The reason seems to lie in the concentration of divine as well as temporal power in the person of the emperor, in China as well as in other oriental societies. The emperor was not only the sole source of political decisions, he was also the Son of Heaven, the representative of the deity among men. . . ."[4]

The *I Ching* views the universe as a natural whole in which change is continual yet connected. Human nature and destiny are closely aligned with universal principles. By studying the *I Ching,* people hope to orient their courses of action within the larger context of harmonious interactions among other people, nature, and the entire cosmos.

The *I Ching* has symbols on it in the form of sixty-four hexagrams, each consisting of six horizontal lines. While some of these lines are solid, others have gaps in their middles. Hexagrams form a circle around hexagrams that form a square. Each hexagram is made of a

---

4. Hellmut Wilhelm and Richard Wilhelm, *Understanding the I Ching: The Wilhelm Lectures on the Book of Changes* (Princeton, New Jersey: Princeton University Press, 1995), page 5. According to Princeton University Press, Richard Wilhelm was the West's foremost translator of the I Ching.

pair of three lone symbols that are called trigrams, and each hexagram has a name. Each trigram has a special meaning, and to learn the meanings, a person studies the *I Ching*, which interprets all the meanings in a series of commentaries. Basically, each hexagram symbolizes particular situations and the hexagram's name refers to these situations, which in turn are described in the *I Ching*.

In the *I Ching* are images about a person's primary needs, his social life, his character traits, and so forth. For example, there are images to represent obstacles, oppression, abundance, the mistakes of youth; a marrying girl, friendship, seeking love, finding love, family, peace, conflict, war; modesty, innocence, truth, enthusiasm; joy, arousal, and gentleness.

Consulting the *I Ching* is much like consulting the Ouija board. First you think of a question about something you intend to do. The question should go far beyond the type of questions that can be answered with Ouija board yes and no movements. For example, you wouldn't want to ask a question such as "Will it rain today?" Instead, you want to think of a question that's more complex.

Dragon Riders have great powers with spells, and in fact, they have so much power they can even bring people back from the dead. Again, we're not told exactly how this might be accomplished, only that it is possible and that magic is the manipulation of the flow of energy.[5]

Perhaps the people aren't really dead yet. Perhaps they're in a zombie state, and the Riders just bring them back from what appears to be death. There is actually some basis in reality to this sort of thing, the notion that a person can be presumed dead, buried in a coffin, then "brought back to life."

In our world, the notion of zombies originated with Haitian Voodoo culture. In fact, the word "zombie" comes from the Haitian word *zombi,* which means spirit of the dead. As the story goes, Voodoo priests called bokors studied enough black magic to figure out how to resurrect the dead using a powder called coup padre.

The primary ingredient of coup padre is deadly

---

5. Paolini, *Eldest,* page 377.

tetrodotoxin from the porcupine fish, the fou-fou. The tetrodotoxin disrupts communication in the brain and is five hundred times more deadly than cyanide. A tiny drop of tetrodotoxin can kill a man.

This weird poison, coup padre, was made by first burying a bouga toad (called a *bufo marinus*) and a sea snake in a jar. After the toad and snake died from the rage of being confined in the jar, the bokor extracted their venom. The toad's glands held bufogenin and bufotoxin, each fifty to one hundred times more deadly than digitalis. The bufogenin and bufotoxin increased the victim's heartbeat. In addition, the glands held bufotenine, a powerful hallucinogenic drug.

To these drugs, the bokor added millipedes and tarantulas to tcha-tcha seeds that caused pulmonary edema, nontoxic consigne seeds, pomme cajou (cashew) leaves, and bresillet tree leaves. (Both of these types of leaves are related to poison ivy.) After grinding everything into a powder, the bokor buried the concoction for two days, after which he added ground tremblador and desmember plants, two plants from the stinging nettle family that injected formic acidlike chemicals beneath the victim's skin; and dieffenbachia with its glasslike needles, which made the victim's throat swell, causing great difficulty in breathing and talking. He then added the sharp needles of the bwa pine.

But we're not done yet . . .

The bokor next added poisonous animals to the deadly powder. Two species of tarantulas were ground up and added to the skins of white tree frogs. Another bouga toad went into the mixture, followed by four types of puffer fish, including the fou-fou carrying the coup padre. The final ingredient was dead human flesh.

If a family or community despised someone sufficiently, they called upon the bokor to turn that person into a zombie.

After ingesting the coup padre, the despised villager or family member immediately became numb. His lips and tongue went numb first followed by his fingers, arms, toes, and legs; then his entire body went numb. He was sick with feelings of weakness, floating, nausea, vomiting, diarrhea, stomach pain, and headaches. Quickly the victim's pulse picked up and he had trouble walking and talking. Finally, paralysis set in:

his breathing became shallow, his heart nearly ceased to beat, and his body temperature plummeted. The victim's body was blue, his eyes were glassy. In essence, the victim was in a coma.

While still alive, the poor, despised victim was buried as if already dead. Because he wasn't really dead, the victim often heard his own funeral and was horrified to suffer through his own burial.

Later, the bokor dug up the body and brought the person back to life. Physically, the person appeared as he did before ingesting the coup padre, but mentally, his mind was gone and his soul was dead. Being traumatized, the victim believed he had been reanimated, or brought back to life. As a mindless drone, this new zombie remained under the bokor's power and did the bokor's bidding. The bokor gave his new zombie a hallucinogenic mixture of Datura stramonium, cane sugar, and sweet potato. There is absolutely no antidote for tetrodotoxin, so once a zombie, always a zombie.

As for teleportation, is it possible for the Shade to transport something instantly from one place to another? Could the elf lady really teleport the large "sapphire stone" from one place to another early in the first novel?

In the real world, teleportation is becoming increasingly possible. In fact, some scientists would say that we can do it already using something called quantum entanglement.

Most simply put, quantum entanglement in the real world means that after two things interact, they always know what's happening with each other. Even when far apart—say, worlds apart—the two things still know instantaneously, just as with a Lodestone Resonator, what is happening at the other end.

Tiny things such as electrons and other particles have waves associated with them. When waves of two quantum particles get tangled, it's called quantum entanglement. If the two quantum particles move far apart, their waves stretch and maintain communication between them. Even if the particles are on opposite sides of the universe. Because we don't have parallel universes—not yet—it's unclear how this might work across universes.

If one atom is split to produce two particles that are

spinning in opposite directions, then those two particles are said to be entangled. If one is horizontally polarized, the other might be vertically polarized.

Experiments have actually shown that two particles with different polarizations can become entangled on opposite sides of a room. When an atom is split and produces two photons that spin in different directions and with different polarizations, those two photons become entangled.

Photons are spin-1 quantum particles traveling at the speed of light, and each photon spins in one direction of motion. If you could see a photon as it approaches you, it might appear to be right- or left-handed, depending on the spin. Notice that we're talking about spin as if the photon is a particle.

As for polarization, it has to do with the wavelike property of light, and it is related to the particle-like property of the photon's spin. According to Maxwell's equations, which we need not explore in depth in this book, a light wave's magnetic and electric fields oscillate at right angles to the direction in which the light is traveling. A photon's polarization refers to the direction in which its electric field is oscillating. Photons can be polarized in many directions, but if a polarizing filter is used (think about sunglasses), the light can be forced into oscillating in specific directions. If a filter is slanted in a particular direction, then the polarization of the photons is slanted in a particular direction.

Using computers to make things happen, scientists change one photon and notice that the other photon does the same thing. For example, a photon flies through a vertical slit and becomes horizontally polarized; instantly, the other photon becomes horizontally polarized.

Using quantum entanglement in 2002, Australian scientists shifted an entire laser beam a distance of one meter. They started with two laser beams, each containing billions of photons that were entangled with photons from the other beam. They poked one laser beam, and all of its photons "jiggled"; and as the photons in the first beam jiggled, the photons in the second beam jiggled, too. Even stranger, when the information about jiggling went from one set of photons to the other set, the entire first laser beam disappeared. It was as if the first laser beam had teleported to a distance one meter away: just like on *Star Trek*.

According to *Nature* magazine in 2001, "a pair of quantum particles can exist in entangled superposition, a mixture of states that resolves only when some physical property such as spin or polarization is measured. Quantum entanglement is a fundamental requirement for quantum computing. . . . Using a new method of generating entanglement, an entangled state involving two macroscopic objects, each consisting of a cesium gas sample containing about 10^{12} atoms, has been created."[6] This work was done by Eugene Polzik at the University of Aarhus's Quantum Optics Center in Denmark. Basically, his team used an infrared beam of light to make a cloud of one trillion atoms of cesium gas assume the quantum spin of another cesium cloud.[7] What this means is that scientists as far back as 2001 were already making larger objects become

---

6. "Quantum Entanglement: Going Large," *Nature* magazine, September 27, 2001, as reported at http://www.nature.com/nature/links/010927/010927-2.html.

7. B. Julsgaard, A. Kozhekin, and E.S. Polzik, "Experimental Long-Lived Entanglement of Two Macroscopic Quantum Objects," *Nature* magazine, Issue 413, 2001, pages 400–403.

entangled, and this entanglement, existing only for 0.5 milliseconds, gave scientists hope that quantum computers and teleportation would someday exist.

Further, says the *Christian Science Monitor,* scientists in Denmark "have entangled two large clusters of atoms in neighboring containers. The feat, the team says, represents the first demonstration of entanglement between separated, large clusters of atoms, at room temperature, and for relatively long periods of time."[8] Earlier, scientists at the National Institute of Standards and Technology in Boulder, Colorado, had entangled four atoms.

Scientists have used entangled photons to transfer money and have commercial hardware to support quantum cryptography.[9] The Swiss company ID Quantique and the American company MagiQ are marketing quantum cryptography, with most customers coming

8. Peter N. Spotts, "Spooky Action at a Distance," *The Christian Science Monitor,* October 4, 2001, as reported at http://www.csmonitor.com/2001/1004/p15s1-stss.html.
9. Mark Buchanan, "Quantum Tricks that Read Your Thoughts," *New Scientist* magazine, December 4, 2004, as reported at http://www.newscientist.com/channel/fundamentals/quantum-world/.

from the military ranks and other government organizations. Quantum computing, in very general terms, uses the various states of photons to represent bits of data. It works along short distances of fiber-optic cable, but scientists hope that quantum repeaters can be used someday to enable teleportation of quantum-based computer data along much longer distances.

Someday, we'll teleport objects without sophisticated laboratory equipment. But whether we will ever be able to hunt and kill other creatures simply by casting spells or thinking is unknown. Whether we will ever be able to use mental telepathy as a major form of communications is unknown. With all of this in mind, we have to remember that what seemed like magic yesterday tends to become tomorrow's science.

· 6 ·

Angela the Herbalist: If Plants Are Conscious, Is She Guilty of Murder?

In *Eldest*, we learn that the elf forest contains a Menoa tree that happens to be "awake and intelligent."[1] Paolini writes that a woman whose lover dumped her became very depressed and sank against the Menoa tree for three solid days and nights. When I get depressed, I don't sink against trees for three days and nights singing like the woman in the *Eldest* story. I'm more likely to sink into my bed and moan. But as

---

1. Paolini, *Eldest,* page 306.

with many subjects in fantasies, the woman singing by the tree is more magical, interesting, and delightful than a woman sinking into bed and moaning.

At any rate, the woman in *Eldest* merges with the tree after three days and nights. (Again, this beats a story about a depressed woman becoming one with her mattress.) The Menoa tree is a magical blending of human, supernatural, and forest.

In real life, can trees be intelligent? At first thought, it seems laughable, doesn't it? But maybe it's not as far-fetched as we think.

According to the *Christian Science Monitor,* "Hardly articulate, the tiny strangleweed, a pale parasitic plant, can sense the presence of friends, foes, and food, and make adroit decisions on how to approach them. Mustard weed, a common plant with a six-week life cycle, can't find its way in the world if its root-tip statolith, a starchy 'brain' that communicates with the rest of the plant, is cut off."[2] Further, claims the *Monitor,* scientists

---

2. Patrik Jonsson, "New Research Opens a Window on the Minds of Plants," *Christian Science Monitor,* March 3, 2005, at http://www.csmonitor.com/2005/0303/p01s03-usgn.html.

believe that all plants, even ferns and flora, are intelligent, speculate about the future, and can conquer enemies and territories. The article quotes Anthony Trewavas, a plant biochemist at the University of Edinburgh in Scotland, who believes that the human definition of intelligence is limited and needs to include the type of thinking that's "much more generally found in life."

Further, recent grants from the U.S. government have been awarded to study plant neurotransmitters, which are assumed by some to be very similar to human neurotransmitters, which are the chemical transmission agents in the brain. At the most basic level, I suppose, where chemicals interact, it's possible. Oxygen and hydrogen combine in the same way to form H_2O whether in a plant or an animal. But we have to keep in mind that plant and animal cells are quite different, and transmissions among these cells have to differ. In other words, it seems extremely unlikely (interpret that phrase as meaning "impossible" but with the slightest touch of the most remote chance) that plants have brains that operate like animal brains and that plants have neurotransmissions that operate like animal neurotransmissions.

Intelligent plants have been featured in a lot of science fiction and fantasy stories. In fact, plants that are merged with humans have been featured in many stories. Murray Leinser's 1935 short novel *Proxima Centauri* features evil tree men as villains who hijack a starship from Earth. David H. Keller's "The Ivy War" from an early issue of *Amazing Stories* describes a mutated ivy plant that takes over a city. In "Plants Must Kill," Frank Belknap Long's space detective John Carstairs battles an intelligent plant that murders businessmen in an asteroid city. In Jack Vance's "The Houses of Iszm," the houses are gigantic, intelligent plants who grow rooms to order. In James Patrick Kelly's award-winning "Mr. Boy," a house made out of super–plant life also serves as a kid's mother. Perhaps the most famous intelligent plant of all is Audrey Jr. from the 1960 B-film (and later musicals), *The Little Shop of Horrors.*

Given that intelligent trees are a staple of science fiction and fantasy, we can easily believe in the magic forests of *Eragon* and *Eldest*. And it helps that Christopher Paolini describes his forests' intelligence in a way that seems aligned with modern thinking. As he writes in *Eldest,* "The plants possessed a different type of consciousness than animals: slow, deliberate, and decentralized, but in their own way just as cognizant of their surroundings as Eragon himself was."[3] Eragon concludes that intelligent life exists everywhere. This is a high point of the novels and opens the possibility that in the third novel, which at the time of this writing hasn't been published yet, we may see more of the world around us: the plants, the stars, the souls. I'm reminded in a slight way of the beauty of Philip Pullman's trilogy *His Dark Materials,* in which the entire world—in fact, thousands of parallel worlds—operate in harmony, with everything imbued with a life force, a soul, intelligence.[4]

Now, if we consider that in Eragon's world, plants are indeed intelligent, then does this mean that Angela

3. Paolini, *Eldest,* p. 538.
4. For a detailed discussion of these subjects, please see my forthcoming book *Exploring Philip Pullman's* His Dark Materials to be published by St. Martin's Press.

the herbalist is a murderer? In fact, if someone eats peas, are they eating a plateful of brains?

Well, the plateful of brains might be a bit silly, but let's face it: in the real world, many people are vegetarians because they don't want to eat other creatures who have intelligence, feelings, nerve endings, pain, neurotransmissions. So, in Eragon's world, are there people who refuse to eat animals *and* plants? If so, what do they eat? Bread is made from plant life. Is there anything nutritional that people can eat for prolonged periods (say, for a lifetime) that does not consist of animal or plant life?

We first meet Angela the herbalist in *Eragon,* where she's surrounded by dried herbs, a mortar, and a pestle. She uses the mortar and pestle to grind the herbs into medicinal remedies. She is a town healer and she has a magic werecat named Solembum.

Among Angela's herbs and potions are other things, such as the knucklebones of dragons, which have enormous power, as well as toadstools, sulphur tuft, dwarf shield, and the spotted deceiver, which causes immediate death. In addition to preparing all the herbs and potions, Angela tells fortunes using tea leaves, crystal balls, and tarot cards. Of course, she predicts Eragon's future, which provides a nice foreshadowing from *Eragon* into *Eldest.*

In the previous chapter, we talked a bit about Voodoo priests and zombies. In essence, these medicine men, or bokor, are herbalists like Angela. They make concoctions out of herbs, animal extracts, and other weird things. Sometimes the concoctions are remedies to heal wounds and make people feel better. Sometimes they cause death or zombielike appearances. Medicine men are town healers, and they are also well versed in the medicine of death.

Herbalists have been around since the beginning of mankind. They're still present in modern days. The next time you are in the grocery store, look for the "natural" remedy section. You'll find aisle after aisle of herbs, potions, and plant vitamin extracts in little jars. Alternative medicine is alive and well.

Hundreds—maybe thousands—of herbal remedies exist in the real world. Angela may be grinding herbs for the townies in *Eragon,* but in our world, she'd be doing the same thing for a large audience. She'd be selling her herbs over the Internet.

Here's a summary of the healing claims of only a few herbs that are in modern use:

- **Abcess Root** (*Polemonium reptans*): Angela would dispense this remedy to treat pulmonary diseases. According to modern lore, abcess root causes people to sweat profusely and will heal ulcerated throats. Some claim that it reduces coughing and helps breathing.

- **Adder's Tongue, English** (*Ophioglossum vulgatum*): Angela might use this leaf to help people who have skin rashes and wounds. She would use oils from the adder's tongue to soothe abrasions and gashes, and she might even make a juice out of it to help treat gout, scurvy, and other diseases.

- **Alumroot** (*Heuchera americana*): This plant contains compounds called tannins that some claim shrink swollen flesh. Herbalists use alumroot to stop bleeding and reduce the inflammation that surrounds cuts and wounds. Because herbs—and in general, plants—contain chemicals that we create as non-botanical medicines, many argue that it makes a lot of sense that the herbal remedies can be used instead of their more "artificial" counterparts. In the case of alum-root, it was actually dispensed at pharmacies in the late 1800s. People used it to treat diarrhea, vomiting, sore throats, and ulcers, as well as bleeding and in-flammation.

- **Broom Snakeroot (*Gutierrezia sarothrae*)**: Western Indians used broom snakeroot to heal insect bites.

- **Bupleurum (*Bupleurum falcatum*)**: This herb has had many uses, among them the treatment of malaria, hemorrhoids, mood instabilities, and various other diseases. In China, it was used as long ago as A.D. 200, but it remains one of the most significant Chinese medicinal herbs. It is believed that bupleurum sucks bad emotions, such as anger and depression, from the body organs.

- **Calendula (*Calendula officinalis*)**: Angela might use this herb to treat headaches and tuberculosis. During the American Civil War, calendula was used by soldiers to stop bleeding, and the ancient Romans used it to treat scorpion bites. Other uses of this herb include treatments for sprains, varicose veins, sunburn, fevers, and athlete's foot. If that were not enough, it's also used to treat cancers and inflammations of internal organs.

· **Cat Thyme** (*Teucrium marum*): Probably, Angela would use a different version known as *Werecat Thyme*. The powder of this herb has been used to treat stomach problems, as well as mental illnesses. We all know that if you eat too many potato chips, you get a stomach ache, and if your stomach hurts too much, let's face it, you *could* go insane. Werecat Thyme supposedly cures both ailments.

Clearly, I could go on and on, listing hundreds of herbs and their uses. But I'll stop with Werecat's Thyme. It's clear that what Angela the herbalist does in *Eragon* is something that is very common in our world.

As mentioned, Angela also tells fortunes using crystal balls, palm reading, and tarot cards. To read palms, she looks at the lines on somebody's hand. In our world, palm reading involves an interpretation of a life line, heart line, health line, and many other lines on the palm. Because it's not a big part of *Eragon* by any means, I won't write much about palm reading here. But as a fun exercise, I'll read my own palm and tell you what the lines say about the author of this book. Here we go. . . .

Read at your own risk:

I have a long and clear life line, but it's cramped rather than swooping. My head line, which is directly above the life line, is deep and straight. My heart line, directly over the head line, is long.

Supposedly, the long life line means that I'm still living where I grew up, that I am "supportive" but hate to move. I live far away from where I grew up, actually, but it's true that I hate to move.

My head line means that logic rules my head, I have a good memory and strong willpower, strong concentration, attention to detail, and strong logical and mental control. The palm reading indicates that I should be more emotional, and good things will come my way. Again, the reading is off. In reality, I'm not at all cold, and if anything, I'm very warm and emotional.

I'm beginning to think that palm reading probably

isn't very successful at determining anything about us. I might choose a crystal ball before believing in a palm reading.

But moving on, the palm reading tells me that my heart line has something to do with the fact that I'm extremely well organized. Since when? I'm incredibly *disorganized.*

As for crystal balls, these are also mentioned in passing by Angela. In addition, the term "scrying" is mentioned in the novels. For example, Eragon uses scrying to see things that are far away or hidden from view. Brom teaches him how to do this using the ancient words draumr kopa.[5]

Scrying comes from another word "descry," which means perceiving. In ancient times, people used mirrors to scry, or see things that were hidden from normal view. If someone didn't have an actual mirror, he might use a bowl of ink shining beneath light or glassware. Polished stones were used, as well as obsidian crystals. The most popular items for scrying happen

---

5. Paolini, *Eragon,* p. 195.

to be mirrors and crystals. Hence, the use of the crystal ball.

If Eragon can scry by uttering ancient words, Angela can scry by gazing into a crystal ball. We're all fascinated by crystal balls. On some level, we *believe.* I happen to have a crystal ball clock radio on my kitchen table. I may have received it for free. I do know that it was very cheap. But it's also very cool. I can utter a question, then press a button on the crystal ball radio and one of half a dozen voices supplies an answer. When I was growing up, a friend had a Magic 8-Ball, and we spent a lot of time asking questions of the ball and *sort of* believing the answers. Of course, we also played with Ouija boards and constructed a fortune-telling booth in front of my friend's house, so the Magic 8-Ball was just part of our joint belief in predicting the future. We also played with handwriting analysis, palm reading, and anything else that seemed cool, spooky, and not of this world. Even today, lots of kids do these sorts of things. Belief in the otherworldly aspects of life, in the supernatural, remains extremely popular. How else do you explain the enormous worldwide popularity of Harry Potter?

As for tarot cards, I've believed in their ability to predict the future since my first tarot reading about twelve years ago. I didn't believe in tarot cards until the reader's predictions came true during the following year. She predicted things I never could have imagined would happen to me. These were life-changing events, huge shocking things, and the tarot cards foretold that they would happen. The reader said she was afraid to tell me what the cards were predicting because it was all so horrible, but at the time, I thought my life was very steady, predictable, and happy. I was happily married, or so I thought, with a couple of children and a pleasant little writing career. The tarot cards predicted that my marriage would end, that I'd be immersed in legal problems for the first time in my life, that I would lose my home, my stability, and much of what was dear to me in the following year. I am sorry to say that the predictions were true.

After that, I believed in tarot cards and started reading them every night to see if my future would get any brighter. I also read the cards to glean advice from them. While the readings comforted me, I never got the same impact during my own readings as I obtained when the "official" tarot card reader predicted my future. She told me that she had a supernatural gift for these things, and hence, she never took money for her readings, as she felt it would be unethical. By contrast, most tarot readers do it for money, and they probably have no supernatural skills whatsoever. I've encountered phonies, and in actuality, the only accurate prediction I've ever witnessed was the first one ever done for me.

All that aside, tarot cards first appeared in the fifteenth century in Italy, and they bore special pictures of the Emperor, the Pope, Death, the Devil, and the Moon. People played a form of bridge called the Game of Triumphs using the tarot cards. The game became popular and spread from Italy into France, and from there, to Austria, Germany, and other countries. It was only much later—in fact, centuries later—that the tarot cards became associated with mystical symbolism.

The reader shuffles the cards and lays them on a flat surface in a particular order. She then turns the cards over in a particular order and interprets their meanings, taken collectively and as individual cards.

If we consider for a moment that all of Angela's methods—palm reading, tarot cards, and crystal balls—work for her, then why does she choose one method over another? I can see that if a guy comes to Angela and he happens to have only burned flesh on his hands, then Angela would not be able to do a palm reading for the guy. She'd have to turn to the crystal ball or the cards. But in general, if she can look into a crystal ball and see the future, why does she need the cards?

As for the character of Angela, she is based on Christopher Paolini's sister, Angela. He writes, "The character of Angela the herbalist has an interesting story. I never intended to have anyone like her in the book, but when Eragon and Brom got to Teirm, I decided to include a lampoon of my sister, who coincidentally is also named Angela. Fortunately for my bodily well-being, she has an excellent sense of humor."[6]

---

6. http://www.teenreads.com/authors/au-paolini-christopher.asp.

· 7 ·

Geography and
Norsemen

Eragon begins with a map of Alagaësia drawn by
Christopher Paolini. Before men and elves existed, dwarves, dragons, and other magical creatures
roamed all over the continent called Alagaësia. Eventually, elves traveled across the sea to Alagaësia, and over
time it became clear that the elves and dragons didn't
like each other very much.

It didn't help, of course, that an elf was stupid and
made the big mistake of killing a dragon. After all, you
don't kill something as huge and powerful as a dragon

and expect that no retaliation will occur, that no other dragons will care, that life will go on as it always did *before* you killed the creature. Obviously, the dragons took revenge and a long war began.

Would a long war start in real life because a person who recently immigrated to a country killed a longtime resident? I suppose it depends on the status of the long-time resident and how hot the subject of immigration happens to be at the moment. In ordinary circumstances, a long war probably wouldn't break out. For example, let's suppose you happen to live in a fictitious country called Algoria, and everyone in Algoria belongs to several fictitious intelligent species, some called the Dracoflavioplatans and others called—oh, let's keep things simple this time!—the Dwarves.

The Dracoflavioplatans and Dwarves frolic about, under no threat from any other intelligent species. They dominate all and peace reigns. Frankly, it's hard to believe that this would actually happen in real life, because even amongst the intelligent creatures of a *single* species, disagreements about food and mates, territorial disputes, greed, jealousy, and other matters come into play. It's hard to believe that the Dracoflavioplatans and Dwarves in our fictitious world don't have disputes with each other and amongst their own races. It's hard to believe that the dragons and dwarves in the earliest times of *Eragon* are never at war on any level.

So, in our fictitious land, along comes another intelligent species, the Elgarahoose. One Elgarahoose, very young and stupid, kills a Dracoflavioplatan—not the king of all Dracoflavioplatans, mind you, but just an ordinary Dracoflavioplatan guy who's on his way to the store for a carton of milk. Instantly, war breaks out among the Dracoflavioplatans and the entire race of Elgarahoose! And the war goes on and on forever.

Somehow, this seems unlikely. If the Dracoflavioplatan happened to be an archduke or king, if he were president of all Dracoflavioplatans, if he were an ambassador, a beloved princess (well, then he wouldn't be a *he*, would *she*?), then it might make sense.

For example, a long time ago in the real world—in June, 1914—General Oskar Potiorek, the Governor of the Austrian provinces of Bosnia-Herzegovina, invited Austro-Hungarian Archduke Franz Ferdinand and his wife, Sophie von Chotkovatao, to watch military maneuvers. Ferdinand happened to be next in line to the Austro-Hungarian throne. So, he wasn't an ordinary guy trekking out for a carton of milk. Up front, of course, Archduke Ferdinand realized that he wasn't being invited to a tea party or an afternoon of playing croquet. He was being invited to watch *military maneuvers*. And it didn't help that the citizens of Bosnia-Herzegovina didn't like their Austrian rulers. In fact, they preferred Serbian rule to Austrian rule, and in 1910, a Serb named Bogdan Zerajic had tried to murder General Varesanin, the Austrian governor of Bosnia-Herzegovina. To make a long story short, Archduke Ferdinand was assassinated, and within weeks Austro-Hungary declared war on Serbia. This war turned into World War I.

In this particular case, the murder was induced by political and military reasons. The person who was murdered happened to be in line for the throne. But had Archduke Ferdinand simply been, say, Ferdinand the Shoe Cobbler, would World War I still have broken out? Probably not. If a stray Serb—not politically aligned with warlike factions—killed a stray shoe cobbler from Austro-Hungary, it would have been news but not world war.

But let's return to Alagaësia, where the dragons and elves hated each other. Their war went on forever and was finally resolved when the first super-powerful super-magical Shur'tugal, a guy named Eragon, was born and rose to young manhood. Eragon made peace between the dragons and elves, and the dragons were so thrilled that they gave the elves several dragon eggs every year so more Dragon Rider teams could exist and maintain the harmony.

Of course, as in any culture where things are terrific, some evil guy has to come along and ruin everything. In Alagaësia, it was Galbatorix, a crazy Rider who went insane. And we all know the story after that.

Alagaësia, then, is a place: a land, just like a country that happens to occupy an entire continent. Five distinct civilizations (but not countries) are in Alagaësia: the Empire, the Varden, the elves, the dwarves, and Surda. Of its seven islands, Vroengard is the most important because the Dragon Riders once lived there. Alagaësia is surrounded by mountains and water, and it is very much tied to the stories of *Eragon* and *Eldest*. In fact, the geography of Alagaësia plays a large role in the books.

The map of Alagaësia at the beginning of *Eragon* shows a vast desert called the Hadarac Desert, which is surrounded by forests and mountains. To the north are the forests, dotted with the names of villages, towns, and rivers. To the west is the Spine, a dangerous mountain range where Eragon finds the dragon egg in the opening scenes.

Possibly due to its enormous size, the Hadarac Desert lies outside the control of the Empire. With Murtagh and (of course) Saphira, Eragon travels through the Hadarac Desert to bring Arya to the Varden.

The treacherous mountains known as the Spine are home to many tales of terror and death. The Spine is considered a "no man's land," dangerous to all. For reasons he doesn't quite comprehend in the beginning of the series, Eragon is able to travel through the Spine without encountering demons, being killed, or going mad. Along with the Hadarac Desert, this is another area that King Galbatorix avoids.

To the south of the Hadarac Desert is another mountain range called the Beor Mountains. Some of the peaks supposedly reach ten miles into the sky, providing more than ample protection for the Varden and the dwarves. A hollow mountain called Farthen Dur is home to the dwarves, and high above Farthen Dur are thousands of icicles known as the Star Sapphire.

As with many role-playing games, the places where Eragon must travel include far more than deserts, waterways, and mountains. Alagaësia includes plenty of villages, fortified cities, and castles. For example, Gil'ead is a fortified city under King Galbatorix's control. Eragon and Arya are captive in Gil'ead, and thankfully, rescued by Murtagh and Saphira.

Teirm, which is near the sea, is also heavily fortified. It is surrounded by walls that are approximately one hundred feet high and thirty feet thick. Soldiers guard the city from atop the wall, and from the distance, people can see the castle of Teirm rising high above the walls. The buildings are shaped like boxes, so men armed with bows and arrows can sit on the flat roof tops and shoot at anyone who displeases them. Bows and arrows, horses, castles, fortified town walls: it all reminds us of knights and medieval times, and of Vikings and Norsemen. As it happens, some scholars believe that Christopher Paolini based his Alagaësian languages and themes on the Norsemen.

The Norsemen spoke a language called Old Norse (which Christopher Paoloni repeatedly says he used as the basis for his elven language) and lived in the remote northwestern region of Europe. According to common myths, these people of the "northern tongue" were driven from their homelands in the southeastern part of Europe by Romans, and they forced their way into Celtic and Finnish societies in Saxland (or Germany) and Scandinavia. Early Norsemen were known as Ynglings or Inglings, and they invaded Celtic Britain, dubbing the country England.

The Norsemen were conquerors and invaded France, Russia, and Holland, calling one particular French province Normandy. The "northmen" who lived in the British Isles during medieval times are often called Vikings. They were ruthless invaders, sweeping in from the seas to kill, steal, and destroy anything and everything. While all Vikings were Norse, it's thought that not all Norse were Vikings—that is, some of the Norse were craftsmen, ironworkers, farmers, and other ordinary folks.

As for castles and bridges leading over water into towns, as for fortified cities: all of these *Eragon* features can be found in Norse and Viking history. For example, the name Trelleborg is given to a set of six forts that double as castles that the Vikings built in Denmark and Sweden. The six castles are Aggersborg in Denmark, Borgeby in Sweden, Fyrkat in Denmark, Nonnebakken in Denmark, Trelleborg in Denmark, and another Trelleborg, this one in Sweden.

Eragon grew up in a village called Carvahall, which lies on the border of the Spine. Brom, Garrow, and other characters live here, as well. Near Carvahall is the town of Therinsford, which lies directly across the Anora River. Utgard, to the slight southeast of Therinsford, is one of the places where the Dragon Riders came in ancient times. In those times, only Dragon

Riders could make it to Utgard, and from there, they would watch over and protect Alagaësia. The feel of the places in *Eragon* is much the same as the feeling of places in medieval northern Europe. In reality, the Norsemen invaded and infiltrated small towns and villages, rode horses through forests and mountains, fought with axes, bows and arrows, and other medieval equipment. While they didn't literally have dragons, they believed in the creatures—just think of the Viking ships with the dragons leading the way!

There's something called the kabbalistic tree of life based on the Hebrew word *sephiroth,* meaning "spheres." The ten sephira are similar to the Norse tree of life. Is it possible that Christopher Paolini came up with Saphira's name based on the Norse or Kabbalistic trees of life?

There's no way to know for sure, but one thing we do know is that had a stupid elf not killed a dragon long ago, the entire continent of Alagaësia would be very different.

· 8 ·
Write Your Own Fantasy

What's a fantasy?

You might say that a fantasy is writing a book when you're a teenager and then seeing it on the *New York Times* best-seller list. However, this particular fantasy is true for Christopher Paolini.

You may have a similar fantasy. Or you may dream of other things, such as trolls and elves duking it out with dragons and hobgoblins in an underground cave. There's probably a point to your fantasy. That is, the fairy creatures aren't just battling for no reason. Most likely, the battle is to remove an evil king, a warlord of some kind, a danger to those who mean no harm to others. In the world of fantasies and fairy tales, good versus evil is the common battleground.

In addition, a good fantasy or fairy tale tries to help us define our own world in more complete ways. We question the standards of our ordinary lives. We realize that we're not alone. There are vast subjects, ideas, possibly creatures and domains all around us that we aren't quite aware of yet.

This is our Fairy Land.

A long time ago, people told each other fairy tales, and eventually these tales were written down and collected into volumes such as *Mother Goose* and *Grimm's Fairy Tales*. Fantasy writers began deriving their own works from these old fairy tales, embellishing the original ideas though often using creatures and settings from the original stories.

Even modern movies borrow liberally from the old fairy tales. Take *Shrek* and *Shrek II* as examples. They feature a princess and an ogre, and they also use fairy tale characters such as Prince Charming and Puss in Boots.

When we're still young, most children believe in magic and fantasy. The notion that there might be elves or talking animals doesn't seem so far-fetched. The idea that your dolls talk to each other and to you at night is fine. The possibility of ghosts seems real.

Somewhere along the way, most adults lose the ability to believe in the magical qualities of life and in fantasy creatures. The popularity of books such as *Harry Potter* gives me hope that adults haven't completely lost their ability to believe in magic, though. The popularity of *Lord of the Rings* and *Eragon/Eldest* are also proof that both children and adults still want to believe that there's something better out there, that good can triumph over evil, that magic might—it just *might*—exist.

Fairy tales and fantasy are important. They lift our spirits, they give us hope. They remind us that there's a chance that things may exist beyond the rigidly defined reality we're taught to see.

If you want to write your own fantasy (and I'm using the terms fantasy and fairy tale interchangeably here), there are a few things you need to consider. But always keep in mind as you contemplate writing your tale that Christopher Paolini succeeded in creating *his* own fantasy books as well as creating magic in his world. Maybe you can do it, too.

A fantasy should have a hero or heroine who goes off on one or more adventures, called quests in video game parlance. Think about Eragon's adventures. They're very similar to role-playing video games involving quests. The hero goes to villages and towns, forests and mountains, and with the help of older wise men, magicians, and magical creatures, the hero finds clues and treasures. The hero obtains more magical powers. He obtains more "health," meaning a longer life. This is all the same as what happens in many fantasy stories, including *Eragon*.

So, here's what you do:

1. Choose a main hero or heroine. You can choose someone like Eragon, who starts as a human and then evolves into an elf later in the story. Or you can choose someone who starts as an elf and later

becomes human. Most fantasies have princesses (*Eragon* has Arya), kings (there's often a dwarf king), and other royalty. You can choose to make your hero an adventurer who has royal blood, or you can make your hero an ordinary guy who somehow becomes royalty. The royalty aspect of your hero isn't critical, of course, but what is critical is that your hero changes during the story. He must learn more about himself. He must be someone your readers will like and admire. This is a very important part of writing fiction of any kind, that your main characters evolve as humans just like real humans grow and learn new things over time.

2. Make sure your main hero or heroine encounters Fairy Land and magic early in your story.

3. Make sure you have plenty of events in your story. Events are different from action sequences such as fights and battle scenes. Events happen, which make the character choose directions, do things, make decisions, act in new and different ways. For example, Eragon's uncle dies so he can't live with him anymore.

Eragon finds the dragon egg, Saphira hatches, and Eragon and Saphira become friends. These are plot events.

4. Any good fairy tale forces the main hero or heroine to make difficult choices. Great risks must be involved. Magic must be used, fairies must be encountered, known, worked with, and disposed of (if they're evil fairies, that is).

5. You can have a happy ending, which most readers prefer, or you can have a miserable ending, in which favorite characters die. For example, in the original "Red Riding Hood," the heroine is consumed by a wolf! Not exactly a happy ending. In the "Three Little Pigs," another wolf eats the main characters. Even in the story "The Three Little Kittens," well, the mother cat slaps her kittens around and basically abuses them because they lose mittens. These are very popular stories, but they definitely aren't lighthearted, amusing tales.

Good luck with your story, and may you be as successful as Christopher Paolini!

· 9 ·
About Christopher Paolini

The formal notes about Christopher Paolini tell us that he was home schooled in Montana and graduated from high school at the age of fifteen, which is when he started writing *Eragon*. At nineteen, he began writing *Eldest*.

His parents self-published *Eragon* and helped Paolini travel around the country to promote his book. He appeared at approximately 130 bookstores, libraries, fairs, and schools dressed in black pantaloons, a red swordsman's shirt, lace-up boots, and a beret.[1] In an interview, he explains how *Eragon* went from a self-published book straight to Knopf/Random House, one of the most significant and respected publishers in the world.[2] While he was in Seattle promoting his self-published *Eragon,* he met Michelle Frey, a Knopf editor, who ended up buying the book and editing it for release by her publishing house. According to the *Christian Science Monitor,* "As it happened, one of those 10,000 [self-published] copies the Paolinis had sold landed in the hands of Carl Hiaasen's stepson, when the family was vacationing in Montana. Hiaasen, author of *Strip Tease* and the Newberry-winning *Hoot,* called his editor at Alfred A. Knopf and suggested the firm might want to take a look."[3]

Paolini says that his favorite character is Saphira, the dragon, who happens to be my favorite character, as well. He writes, "As I wrote Saphira, I made her the best friend anyone could have: loyal, funny, brave,

1. http://www.csmonitor.com/2003/0807/p20s01-bogn.html.
2. http://www.teenreads.com/authors/au-paolini-christopher.asp.
3. http://www.csmonitor.com/2003/0807/p20s01-bogn.html.

intelligent, and noble. She transcended that, however, and became her own person, fiercely independent and proud."[4]

Paolini no longer wears medieval costumes when he appears on stage. As CNN puts it, "When Christopher Paolini walks on the high school stage for his book-signing appearance, wearing jeans and carrying a black backpack, he could be mistaken for a student. But he gets a rock-star reception from his fans, with wild cheers and flashing cameras."[5]

As I write this book, Paolini is twenty-one years old and working on his third novel in the Inheritance trilogy. A movie of *Eragon* is being filmed in Hungary with John Malkovich and Jeremy Irons in lead roles. Within the first week of release, more than 425,000 copies of *Eldest* sold, and the first print run was 1.8 million copies, most or all of which will probably sell. Indeed, *Eragon* has already sold 2.5 million copies and has been a number-one *New York Times* best-seller, a

4. Ibid.
5. http://www.cnn.com/2005/SHOWBIZ/books/09/28/books.christopher.paolini.ap/index.html, September 25, 2005.

number-one *Publishers Weekly* best-seller, and a *USA Today* best-seller.

It's all pretty amazing, and as the *New York Times* sums up *Eragon*: "[It's] an authentic work of great talent."[6]

But you guys already know that, don't you?

See you at the theaters when *Eragon,* the movie, is released!

---

6. http://www.alagaesia.com/eragon.htm, also quoted on the book jacket of *Eldest.*